CW00363104

Eva Cox was born in Vienna just before Hitler took over in 1938. She spent the war years in England with her mother and, after two years in Rome, arrived in Sydney aged ten. A refugee and an outsider, Eva coped by questioning authority. She became a feminist at the age of three when denied the chance to play the drums in the school band because that 'was only for boys'!

Eva started University in the 1950s and discovered politics, the Sydney Push and University revues. She completed a BA Hons at the University of New South Wales in the 1970s as a mature age, sole parent, and became a founding member of the Women's Electoral Lobby in New South Wales in 1972. Eva has worked as an academic, director of a major non-government welfare organisation, a ministerial adviser, a senior public servant, and has run her own business. She is currently lecturing at the University of Technology, Sydney.

Eva lives on a hill in Glebe, an inner Sydney suburb, with a view of city buildings and boardrooms. She is worried that she is becoming respectable: in 1995 she was awarded an AO in the Queen's Birthday Honours and delivered the ABC Boyer Lectures. Entitled 'A Truly Civil Society', they described Eva's view of the changes needed in society. This book details her ideas on how we can all share in creating the futures we want.

# Leading
# Women

## EVA COX

RANDOM HOUSE
AUSTRALIA

Random House Australia Pty Ltd
20 Alfred Street, Milsons Point, NSW 2061

Sydney   New York   Toronto
London   Auckland   Johannesburg
and agencies throughout the world

First published in 1996
Copyright © Eva Cox 1996

All rights reserved. No part of this publication may be reproduced, stored in a
retrieval system, or transmitted in any form or by any means, electronic,
mechanical, photocopying, recording or otherwise, without the prior written
permission of the Publisher.

National Library of Australia
Cataloguing-in-Publication Data

Cox, Eva.
Leading women.

Includes index.
ISBN 0 09 183070 2.

1. Women executives. 2. Leadership. 3. Success in
business. I. Title.

658.409082

Text design by Liz Nicholson
Cover design by Phillip Campbell
Cover photo by Lorrie Graham
Typeset by Midland Typesetters, Maryborough
Printed by Griffin Paperbacks, Adelaide

Eva Cox makes two things plain in this exuberant book. First, that a world with lots of leading women would be a far more civilised and interesting place. Secondly, that Eva herself is not a 'difficult' woman but a very wise one. In Vienna, where we both were children, she'd be called a *Mensch*!

Robyn Williams

This is a strong and thoughtful book about an important subject. Why is the public arena—which affects so much of our lives—still dominated by powerful men? And why, despite all our advancements, are there still so few women as leaders? Eva Cox, as wise and provocative as ever, blames neither women nor men, but analyses the causes and leads us to some solutions.

Anne Deveson

Vintage Eva—lateral thinking, risk taking, persuasive writing, unassailable experience and at last in a package for all of us. I loved it for all these reasons plus its Australianess.

Wendy McCarthy AO

Move over Mary MacKillop, here comes a secular saint.

Phillip Adams

# Contents

# Acknowledgments

This book is offered as my contribution to a feminist future. Even though there are times in the text where I am critical of some women and the way we sometimes act, this is a critique from within the movement. So, to the ever vigilant media looking for splits and conflicts, sorry but I am not giving up on feminism.

I want to publicly thank the women who provided skills for the gestation of this book, thus making it possible: my daughter, Rebecca, who reorganised the early draft and made clear what I was saying; my friends who talked through the ideas with me; my editor Bernadette Foley; my assistant Catherine Myson; and my agent Lyn Tranter. They listened and supported me through some very sticky moments—this is powerfully feminist!

# Introduction

Do you trust today's leaders?

Have you ever wanted to change their decisions?

Have you ever wanted to make a difference but been too afraid to speak up?

How comfortable do you find the idea of power?

Can you see yourself as a leader?

Think about your reactions to these questions. How do you feel about leadership; about your possible involvement? No one is going to tally your answers but I hope that you will come to understand your reactions and perhaps some of your views will change as you read on. You may also decide to put into practice some of the ideas suggested in this book.

This is a book about women's often uneasy relationship with leadership and power. In writing it I have used my long experience as a researcher, my training as a sociologist and my involvement as an activist advocate. The result is not an academic treatise, but more like a long discussion we might have in someone's living room, or a workshop where we spend time teasing out ideas and feelings about what has happened and what we can make happen. It is about ideas and ways of seeing the world.

I draw on very wide readings, listening to the radio, watching TV and films, talking to people, and on what I have personally done and seen. Writing it has been fascinating as I have explored laterally a half-century of living and observing, testing my ideas against experience and years of social research.

This book is like a mosaic that I have created by making patterns from half-glimpsed images, and by putting together pieces of apparently unrelated ideas and incidents. With these in place, I can map ways of making changes, using the patterns to see how problems might be solved.

In many ways this book is my story, and the story of other Australian women who have made a difference over the last twenty years to the way our world works. I am a passionate reformer. I am not always sure which way to go, but I want to leave the world a better place for my having been here. Many other women share this desire, but traditionally women's roles have been limited to the home and private spheres. For centuries the public arena has been the domain of powerful men, yet this is the area which affects so much of our lives.

## Introducing myself

It is now almost 25 years since I became active in the women's movement and a public advocate of social change. A small group of us started working in the early 1970s for change and for more women to be involved in the broad political system. Maybe we were 'special', because we were the first to find our voices and power in a time of reform, because we were using the banked-up anger that had grown from being discriminated against and through missed opportunities or from being put down. We were known as second-wave feminists; the first wave had brought us the vote, amongst other reforms, in the early twentieth century.

As the earliest groups of second-wave Australian feminists we made an important mark on politics, policy and social structures. These reforms have been visible and substantial, so that the worlds of our children are very different to the worlds we grew up in, just as our lives are radically different from those of our parents. Some of the changes are small but significant, like desegregating employment advertisements; some, such as making sex discrimination illegal, are of more import.

Many of the changes that were set in place in the 1970s have been added to since then. New issues such as domestic violence are now on the agenda, more women are now in non-traditional jobs, in Parliament and the senior executive areas. We have had, and still have, overtly feminist government ministers and even state premiers. We have been successful in putting the issues that we mobilised around in the 1970s, such as child care, onto the agenda of the major political parties. We have even joined some parties to implement change. We can count many victories achieved in the structuring of government policies and have gained services in areas where once there were none.

We were convinced that the reforms we sought would benefit women, and most of them did. However, the last two decades have seen many other changes that are not necessarily positive.

We also bequeath the next generation many structures that have become more entrenched and resistant to positive change.

We need seriously to consider why women still face many of the abiding inequities and problems they do, and why today's decision makers appear to be even more removed from the practicalities and realities of women's lives. What seems to be occurring is a devaluing and diminishing of women's views and experiences rather than an increasing legitimacy for them.

This does not mean that there are fewer women in senior positions. In fact the opposite is true, but although there are more of us, our influence is arguably no greater. There are still not enough of us and at the rate we are going there may never be: Carmen Lawrence commented that worldwide, the number of women politicians has dropped from 14 per cent to 11 per cent.[1] Leonie Still, a management academic, notes that the proportion of women in senior positions in the private sector is also falling.[2]

While we have worked to bring women's views and issues into the system, other changes have occurred in the socio-political landscape that further isolate many of the issues we are raising. While women put new items on the public agenda, other groups are working to downgrade the role of governments and to reduce the number and scope of the activities that were once seen as the legitimate concern of the public sector.

It is men's issues—the validation of economic measures and public markets—which dominate national and international agendas. It is still mainly men whose views and experiences are reflected in the big decisions made in politics and business. The dominant masculinity of these concerns makes the presence of a few women of little consequence when it comes to changing the agenda.

It is important to recognise however, that what are often labelled 'women's issues' are, in fact, general issues which masculine institutions and culture do not see as their responsibility. Men too have children and aging parents, yet solving problems such as these is still seen as women's 'responsibility'. The net gains and losses of the past two decades probably puts us in front in terms of gains for women, but maybe we are losing ground in the macho culture of 'competition' and through cuts to government programs. I have found that mine is not a popular view.

I am in a peculiarly apt position to write this book as I am a committed feminist, but one who has maintained a persona as independent critic. I now hold no political appointments nor do I work as a public servant, though I am an academic. I am past the age where I have to worry about 'having a career'. I identified my fiftieth birthday as the time I could stop being 'promising' and relax. And I have plenty of practice at catching flak and saying both the unexpected and sometimes unpopular.

I can't claim I enjoy this last experience. Like most people I prefer praise, admiration and acceptance. It is just that I have never been very good at working the system to gain these responses, so I have decided I might as well enjoy my role as independent critic. This is, no doubt, a product of my background. I am an outsider, a viewer from the edge, a refugee with a somewhat peripatetic childhood. One of the first times I felt a sense of belonging was when I became actively involved in feminism. The early days of the 1970s offered camaraderie and the excitement of discovering other women like myself. For the first time I was able to share many of the disquiets I felt were mine alone.

By age ten I had been through two continents, three languages and four countries. I became stateless less than three weeks after my birth in Vienna in 1938. At thirteen months I went from being part of a well-off family to being a desperately poor refugee, and from being surrounded by family and people I knew to being alone with my mother in a foreign country. It is not an unfamiliar story for those born Jewish in Austria just before the outbreak of World War Two.

What it meant for me was that by the age of ten I had already experienced years of not fitting in, of being an outsider, of not belonging. I was constantly working the different rules as the games changed around me. This left me with an abiding desire always to question how the world worked; I had to know in order to survive the constant strangeness of a shifting environment. These experiences have also left me another legacy: the passion to work for change when I believe it is necessary. The outsider looking in sees more than the insider, and by the age of three I was already existing both inside and outside the process. Learning the rules intentionally, rather than just absorbing them, makes them visible. Like learning another language, the process reveals the grammar and improves the understanding of your own vocabulary and voice.

I made some deliberate choices at various stages to remain on the margins because the view was better and the freedom to comment is something I value. At other times I wanted to belong, to receive recognition and be part of the crowd, but I have never been very good at following what I often regard as ridiculous rules.

My feminism started at a very early age: a teacher working at the Sunshine Kindergarten in war-torn England has a lot to answer for. When I was three years old, she explained to me at my first session with the percussion band that I could not have a cymbal or drum as they were only for boys. She handed me a very tinkly triangle and said I could aspire to a tambourine. I still remember my anger at the unfairness of it all.

My father probably reinforced my early combative tendencies by modelling some of the best and worst aspects of a committed world saver. He would often greet people with a question on what they had done that day to make the world a better place. This embarrassed me grossly as a child and adolescent, but imprinted on me political commitment. He probably also gave me models of how to constantly question and stir, which have not always been to my advantage or comfort.

My chequered career involved me in many facets of the system: stints working for government ministers and other politicians, for public services, for lobby groups, and for myself. Like many women of my generation, I rose rapidly and went further in jobs and the public eye than I imagined was possible. I became a public figure, a media performer, and moved into influential positions. I committed myself to social change and saw the jobs in which I was employed primarily as a means to this end.

And there's the rub. Sometimes, when I played an insider's

role, I found an institutional lack of will to allow me to use my capacities appropriately—I was seen as threatening the status quo. By pushing for change and challenging authority I breached many rules, both explicit and implicit. In most cases I knew what I was doing and did it deliberately, but there were times when I was not fully aware. These related most often to perceived breaches in manners, or in interpersonal skills; both of which translate as failing to play the game in a feminine style.

Behaviour of this type has made me a target for criticism. This is painful as, like most women, I seek approval, especially from other women. Sometimes I was puzzled by being treated as a form of ideological Typhoid Mary: a carrier of dissenting views which had to be devalued to avoid others being infected. At other times, there was a certain familiar comfort in being an outsider looking on.

Women are rarely valued for speaking out, for their strength of will or their risk taking. Their rewards come from conformity, compliance and comfort. So how does it happen that some of us escape the process and become outsiders? I have often wondered where I went 'wrong' or was it 'right'? Whatever the cause, the position of outsider goes back a long way, probably to my childhood. I have often functioned from the margins somewhat idiosyncratically.

I missed out on certain common forms of Anglo-cultural, female socialisation. I use conflict as a tool for raising issues; I confidently speak out on a wide variety of issues; I have many ideas and I want to share them; I tend to focus on these ideas, not people, and need to think things through rather than feel them.

Reading this list, I wonder why these traits seem so negative. Is it deviant to be outspoken, to argue for what you believe in, to be one of the first to speak, to have lots of ideas and want to share them? Why should these be so unusual in women that we look for causes as though it is pathological? This leads me to question the definition of 'difficult women' and makes me realise that most of us in this catagory have had to buck the feminine stereotype.

I want to know why so few women have made it through the system. So being a sociologist as well as an activist, I use my reading, research and personal experiences to make an amalgam and create some explanations which help me both to understand the world and suggest ways to change it. What I write comes from my work as a trainer and my research into women and skills. It is also filtered through my extensive personal experiences in the various institutions that control our lives: political parties, community groups, universities, advocacy groups, the public service; and running a small business.

This is a not another book on women and leadership that promises recipes for success. In the current climate such formulas are just about joining the system by fitting in. If you find the present system unacceptable for personal and/or political reasons, I hope this book will help encourage you to change it.

## Contradiction of feminine leadership

Can we expect a feminist leadership? I think we can if we redefine what we mean by feminist and feminine, and move on from the current narrow definitions, which seem to exist mainly to control us. These terms are often seen as negative and usually stereotype our attributes into cartoon characters. We also need to ask, what are the alternative ways of seeing leadership, and how can we make these more comfortable for women?

We shouldn't want to be leaders simply because we have a right to be, nor avoid leadership just because we don't want to lead. Women need to take on this role because our contribution will improve the quality of leadership.

I am worried that so few women are putting their views forward and making their voices heard. Even counting all those outspoken women I see and hear, including those who would disagree with much of what I say, we are still a surprisingly small minority. This is accepted as 'natural', so that few even comment on it. Currently women make up: 3 per cent of board directors; 12 per cent of politicians in lower houses; 15 per cent of public sector senior executives—fewer in the big corporations; one Federal Cabinet minister; and so on. And our numbers are not increasing with any regularity.

In this book I refer primarily to Australia, but also to the other English-speaking countries: New Zealand, the UK, USA and Canada. My perceptions are that these countries have become more internally divided, more individualistic, less concerned about in-equalities and disadvantage, and more fearful of their futures. Sticking within these generalities, I believe that the present lead-erships in these countries show neither adequate imagination and ethics nor visions for the future to give me confidence in their ability to lead. The leaders are nearly all men who work within a narrow confine of experience and views, and within particularly limiting masculine stereotypes of what is and is not important. I have written this book to help women recognise the possibilities of power and the need to become involved.

Leading women? We need more, many more, leading women: women in positions of influence and power. When I drafted the outline for this book I wrote the words 'leading women', then said them out loud. I realised they could be interpreted as referring both to women as leaders and to women being led, as in 'are you part of the team leading women into the wilderness?' The ambiguity in the term reflects the dilemma facing many women.

Why aren't more women leading as well as being led? We should all be concerned that so few women become leaders of organisations which can, and do, substantially influence the way the world works. How can the current crop of leaders (which is largely male) make decisions about our futures without our input? Women are needed to extend the abilities and experiences of male leaders so that decisions reflect what we all, women and men, want for the world.

My focus here is on formal leadership, the people who control the institutions, which in turn affect the way society is run. These institutions may be international, national, regional or local; government or non-government; business or public sector, and are institutions of influence and control so their leaders count.

Some feminists question this approach. They feel that an emphasis on senior women or women as leaders is about individual power and success, so see this as the wrong focus. They argue instead that feminists should concentrate on the women at the bottom who lead desperate lives and need immediate help.

I do not devalue or ignore the need for grassroots work, for informal leadership at local levels and the work behind the scenes. I recognise the need for action at all levels, but I feel we too often ignore those areas traditionally deemed to be male preserves.

Other feminists claim that the existing leadership structures are too aggressive, too masculine to be tolerated, and that women in power are corrupted by the money and glamour of life at the top. I acknowledge both concerns and want to make it clear that my interest in women in powerful roles is not focused on their salaries and status, but on their capacity to change leadership directions and ultimately benefit the women at the bottom.

I realise there are risks. There is evidence on both sides of the argument about what differences women can make at senior level. We have Margaret Thatcher as a constant reminder that women are neither necessarily softer nor more caring in the policies they push. On the other hand, we have the example of Norway, where a very feminised Cabinet has created considerable change in its agenda, albeit not a revolution.

Women need to be leaders, to have input, and to take responsibility for the results as fully adult beings. I go to conferences of women and see delegates attending as passive spectators, as observers, but not as active participants. There are a few of us always ready to speak, and a few younger ones wanting to join us, but there are too many who wait and see.

## How do we lead?

This book is in three parts. Part One outlines the different contributions we can make to leadership: to making things happen, to changing the way the world works. In this section I ask, is there a better model of power than the present ones that are built on affirming and rewarding traits which are gendered masculine, when they do not work for many men as well as women?

It is not that women do not possess these traits, but rather that when we exhibit them we are often labelled unfeminine. Of course, for most women it is not that we are passive or dependent, for example, but rather that we experience aggressiveness or autonomy in different measures and situations to men. It is not surprising to find then that corporations, governments and institutions—which for many years have been dominated by men—have gendered assumptions about what makes a 'good' worker built into their cultures.

This is why we need to review the nature of leadership and the power of institutions. As women we too often fall into the stereotypes and become merely reactive, so that we fail to recognise that our discomfort or feelings of inadequacy come from behavioural definitions made within masculine paradigms. Men too are often not suited to these paradigms, which reward only particular forms of masculinity.

In Part Two I look at ways to identify how we sabotage our own efforts and those of other women. We may not be our own worst enemies but we certainly assist when we internalise and reproduce discrimination. By judging ourselves and other women by rules we haven't had a say in making, we act as agents of social control to restrict the activities of women.

Those who identify with, or are validated by, the current models act as gatekeepers for them, but more surprisingly, so do many women who would see themselves as change agents. These women often do not recognise their own complicity in this process of denying other women power.

Finally, in Part Three I ask, how do women as individuals or groups overcome the problems? Are there other forms of leadership that work better? The third part of this book looks at some practical options that women can use both to rethink leadership, and work out ways to take it on. If we move past the masculine and feminine models, what can we find that recognises both the diversities and strengths of women and men?

## Doing it to ourselves

What is new in this book is a feminist inside view of what women do to each other in formal organisations and semi-formal groups. I know this is dangerous ground as the media is always interested in covering political movements as though we were sporting teams. Those committed to what I call 'women-on-women mud wrestling stories' will try to set up the second part of the book as a story of the conflict within feminism. That is not the point I am aiming to make. Rather I am trying to examine how we are implicated in the processes that we also fight against.

Writing this book has been a bit like following a detective story. I have looked for clues, patterns, odd relationships and anomalies in many disciplines and places. As I read, talked and wondered, I became aware that as women we need to look at what we do to ourselves and each other to block our own progress. In other words, women have to stop acting as though we are passive victims, even though we are in a framework of power which is defined primarily by men.

I do not want to undermine what other women (and I) have done, or are doing. I am, however, increasingly concerned that we are being confined in numbers and in areas of influence both externally and by our own responses to these pressures. So I am taking the risk of saying publicly what many have said to me in private.

Feminists have focused so often on what men do to us that we have written little on what we do to ourselves. How do we need to change? It is going to be tough. This is not a book of easy solutions, with a few prescriptions for success. It's about how women can change the way we operate to become leaders and how we can encourage and support other women who want to do so. What you are reading is designed to be useful to you as an individual, but it is also very much about the ways we connect and are responsible for each other.

This book is the bittersweet account of how women must change or else remain, in part, responsible for our failures. Unlike the fairy tales, there is no necessary happy ending and virtue may not be rewarded. Even if women follow the recipes for success, individually or in groups, many may still fail, because the problems out there are not ones we can solve easily or individually.

Within these limits, the book is a practical guide on how to, and how not to, make it into leadership roles at all levels. But it needs to be read with an understanding that power is not merely personal. This means there should be no individual guilt or blame if women try and fail, because we know it is tough out there. So have a go, because if women do not try because it hurts too much to fail, we all lose.

If you are a woman who wants to see changes and wonders how to bring them about, read on. If you are one of the men who understand that tapping women's skills will make the world a better place, read on too, but be warned that some of what men have done is under scrutiny and will be criticised.

We cant all be followers..
Someone has to lead.

## CHAPTER 1

# What is Power?

The *Concise Oxford Dictionary* defines *power* as the ability to do or act, a particular faculty of mind or body; from the Latin *posse*—be able.

'Don't start with power', suggested Edna Ryan, when she read the first draft of this book. 'It is too confronting!' As one of our senior feminists, she has had over seventy years of active involvement to work out what women want. 'And when you are talking about women in power', she added, 'don't forget to acknowledge that those who support them are also just as necessary'.

Sensing and owning our own power are not experiences many women share or find familiar. Instead we are often socialised to share pain and develop forms of resistance to perceived male power. Few women learn to deal with risk taking or are encouraged to develop the belief that we can do what we want by and for ourselves. Thus for a majority of women, the concept of power is both alienating and alien.

A feminist anthropologist, told of the topic of this book, provided an example: 'We don't want to talk about power!' she said sternly. The implication was that I was discussing something antithetical to feminism. The word *leadership* also evokes negative reactions from many avowed feminists because of its association with power.

The relative absence of either power or leadership in feminist discussions, writings and political claims is noticeable and notable. I went through my not inconsiderable library, using the indexes to look for the terms *leadership* or *power*. Within most of the feminist publications there were few entries for those words and often none at all, even when the topics were ostensibly political.

A recent book about senior women in the media industry, published in the UK, is entitled *The Executive Tart and Other Myths*,[1] and lists only five index items under *power*. Another UK book, *Womanwords*,[2] which lists 300 woman-related keywords, has no mention of *power* or *leadership* and none of their synonyms.

To understand the common usages of the word *power* I looked in my software's thesaurus. Thesauruses are often more telling than dictionaries as synonyms give us a sense of where words are positioned and whether the words carry within them any gender baggage.

## Power

1. Force, might, potency, strength, energy, stamina, vigour, authority, command, control, domination, omnipotence.

Most of these words are associated with masculine attributes to the point where some of them, when coupled with *woman* (for example, controlling woman, dominating woman, forceful woman) are pejorative. Most suggest and tend to represent power over another person.

2. Ability, capacity, faculty, potential, skill.

These are more likely to be attractive as they are about having power to do, or to act, rather than power over another.

## Authority

1. Critic, expert, judge, master, specialist.

These words all assume forms of recognised expertise and are obviously defined by whether the knowledge itself is regarded as legitimate. Many areas in which women have expertise are not seen to be authoritative.

2. Command, control, government, rule.

These are terms that cover a legitimated, and often legal, role.

3. Influence, might, strength.

Power here is pretty straightforward; it's about force.

When I looked up *masculine* the synonyms suggested were 'powerful', 'robust' and 'strong', while *feminine* offered 'dainty', 'delicate' and 'soft'.

This crudely illustrates one of the major barriers that face women attempting to adopt aspects of power and influence; they can only be unfeminine.

Power in early second-wave books was often seen as personal and related to oppression in gender relationships. Hester Eisenstein in *Contemporary Feminist Thought*,[3] stated her concern that: 'a feminist analysis which locates power only in individual psychology is both naive and damaging', and I agree.

Generally when power is mentioned in feminist publications

it is defined as 'power over' rather than 'power to'. It is associated primarily with the negative experiences of victims. Therefore the associations are with oppression, whether by individual men, or by institutions run on masculine lines.

Power in political theory is somewhat more complex, involving concepts of authority and force. It is defined as the ability to exact compliance or obedience; authority is defined as a recognition of the competence of the individual and/or the office they hold, often governed by rules and laws; force is compulsion by use of violence or fear of violence, usually invoked to support power and authority.[4] It is interesting that the *Oxford Dictionary* shows similar origins for the words *authority* and *author*, which are about originating and promoting ideas, moving to power. Maybe we need to adopt *authority* as the term of preference as it seems less imprinted with coercion and more with leadership by knowledge.

However, were we to use this less threatening term, I suspect we would end up with the word itself being devalued, as women will be allowed authority but men will retain their power. There are limits to using euphemisms, in trying to soften and sanitise language, when the underlying problem remains.

I decided that I needed to do some reading on theories of power. Max Weber, a German sociologist,[5] identified three types of authority. The first two were: traditional, drawing from history, for example, the monarchy or tribal elders; and charismatic, deriving from personal or religious emotive appeal, for example, Hitler or various evangelists.

These forms of authority still operate at many levels,

including within local communities and families. They are often informal but nevertheless recognisable.

The final type was rational-legal authority, which is the one I am most interested in here. Rational-legal authority is codified and accepted by the society in which it functions, for example, in most modern governments and executive arms of businesses. These codes came about with the development of modern State and political systems. They sought to replace traditional, often face-to-face relationships, with laws and rules which in theory created impartial decision making. These codes are the source of modern bureaucratic systems of power and influence.

All three of Weber's types of authority depend on being legitimated, that is, actively accepted by those deemed to be 'powerless'. This is important because it recognises that it is very difficult for those in authority to sustain coercive power without some cooperation from the society over which they govern.

These definitions are about formal, top-down power which involves three basic assumptions: power is possessed, for example, by individuals or by a class; power flows from a centralised source from top to bottom, for example, law, economy, State; and power is primarily repressive in its exercise, that is, it imposes prohibitions and sanctions.

In more recent theory there has been some movement away from the top-down institutional concept of power and oppression into a more shifting and amorphous construct. This is epitomised in the work of Michel Foucault, a French philosopher, who describes power as a fluid process which is identified through examples of interactions rather than any clear, overall process. He claims one cannot look at the power of institutions as such, but that true power reveals itself in the micro power relations, person to person, that exist and make other power possible. His definition says that:

*power is exercised not possessed*

*power is not primarily repressive, but productive*

*power comes from the bottom up.*[6]

Foucault claims the ownership of power creates a debate about legitimacy, consent and rights which opens up possibilities of other powers. In the Introduction to a recent book, *Transitions: New Australian Feminisms*, the editors Barbara Caine and Rosemary Pringle[7] quote Elizabeth Grosz's definition of power: 'power can be thought of as running around and through us, like honey, in various states of fluidity and congealment'.

Later in the Introduction, Caine and Pringle translate power as violence.[8] This reduces the meaning of power so that it can only ever be bad, rather than acknowledging the possibilities of women (and men) using power to achieve positive ends. In this book, I attempt to redefine and use power as a beneficial social change agent, without overlooking the potential of its darker side.

In Women's Studies courses there is little coverage of power in the political sense. The concerns here are more likely to reflect an interest in the interpersonal not the formally institutional. I have problems with this as I have seen the tendency of governments, political parties, unions and employers to ignore their roles of influence. There is a separate and substantial literature on women in management. These books and how-to guides emphasise individual success, or the benefits for managers of having women in the system. Their use of the term *power* is different but not particularly helpful here—power breakfasts, power walking, power dressing. Power has also been promoted in the personal growth area and the book trade has caught up with its sales potential. Naomi Wolf's best-seller *Fire with Fire* is subtitled *The New Female Power and How It Will Change the 21st Century*. Clarissa Pinkola Estes' *Women Who Run with the Wolves* has as a subtitle *Contacting the Power of the Wild Woman*.

The sales of Wolf and Pinkola Estes are high enough to suggest that many women, in the privacy of their reading, indulge in some personal power fantasies. I am not convinced however, that these translate into any substantial form of personal or political action as the contrary indications are still all around us.

I first noticed the discomfort some women experience in acknowledging any desire for power or leadership when I was running training programs for the Australian Public Service. These were for women who were potential entrants to the Senior Executive Service. By definition at least, the women were relatively powerful, but power and leadership were not concepts with which they were comfortable.

In these workshops the mention of the words power and leadership usually resulted in a physical response. When they could, the women would move their chairs back from the table and turn their bodies side-on so they could, at least metaphorically, leave the discussion. Other women, who are also involved in training women as managers, often report the same phenomenon in discussions I have had with them. For many women, these two terms are so identified with certain masculine values that they find it difficult even to discuss them.

## Power and leadership—do we need them?

My answer is yes. Women need them and we want them as long as we don't have to be too obvious or threatening in achieving them. Women want to influence the way we live and the lives of others around us. A study in Queensland[9] showed that women were not different to men in wanting senior positions at work. We are not backwards in telling people what we do not like, so presumably we want these problems fixed.

We need power to bring about these changes. We must also decide that we can act on our own behalf. This is very hard at an individual level and often far too frightening. So, many women realise that they cannot cope with the process and stay where they are because it is comfortable, or at least familiar. We cannot bring about major reform as individuals; social change is something we need to work on together.

Women have the prerequisite of leadership, which is the desire to have some impact. The puzzle is why women are so ambivalent about becoming part of the process of change. Is it the term *leader*? Has it been appropriated within such a stereotypical male image that it puts most women off? Is there an image of jackboots and uniforms, or sporting heroes, or of politicians who exude a particular kind of self-confident infallibility to which women cannot relate?

There are few who would disagree that women should take our share of the responsibility for running the world: in big or small business, politics, media, the arts, the community, and all other areas of power and influence. But how do we get into these positions? Also, and this is crucial, how do we take on the responsibilities that go with the rights we have already claimed? These are hard realities women must face.

Without access to power, we risk losing many of the gains women have made over the last century. In that time, in English-speaking countries, we have been asking for our share. We have had the vote since 1895 in South Australia and federally since 1902. However, it took us a long, long time to get women into Parliaments, and even longer to make it into Cabinet and leadership roles. Our first Federal members were elected in the 1940s and we have never had more than one woman at a time in Cabinet in Canberra.

If we want to achieve the changes that are proposed to political representation, for instance, or in management, we need to be ready to make and take the opportunities. Women must also support other women to gain leadership roles and keep them.

In the past, when we were formally excluded from power in our society, we were also protected from needing to take on the attendant responsibilities. Now that we have broadened our options we have to be prepared for the obligations these entail.

There are plenty of good and bad arguments we can put forward, blaming all women's woes on men. These then underrate and overlook the power of women. We may not have caused many of the problems we face, but we must take responsibility for finding solutions. Let's move the debate from the idea that women are simply and unilaterally oppressed by men and recognise some responsibility for our own position.

## Women and power possibilities

The discussion of women's 'oppression', as mentioned above, implies a one-way process of pressure. This puts women into a powerless, victim position which suggests that we have no agency in our own lives. I believe that this oversimplifies the complexities of relationships both individual and institutional, and undervalues the contributions women make to them.

If we assume that power is a two-way process we have to recognise that women are actively part of this process, albeit unequally. We may be restrained by a range of factors, so we feel unable to act on our own behalf, and may actually be severely constrained by our circumstances. There may be physical force, or threats, or economic problems which inhibit our ability to act as we might want. Also, our behaviour is confined by what are seen as appropriately feminine responses.

We are taught that being feminine is to be compliant, good natured, nurturant and supportive. On the other hand, showing anger, resisting or rejecting what is acceptable, is not seen as appropriately feminine. Women are expected to accept their lot and deal with it. This is the message of our mothers and their mothers.

However, some women have choices even within these constraints, and opportunities to resist and transgress. Therefore, our actions and inactions must be seen as part of the process and subject to discussion. This raises the concept of agreement, of consent, and also raises complex issues about the interaction of dominance and submission.

While one can question whether there can be an acceptable contract between people who are unequal in power, there are obvious levels of consent and resistance. I fully recognise the serious difficulties women face in changing what they see as oppressive or violent behaviour, particularly when there are threats or violence.

Compliance is agreeing to something whether or not the person who consents has sufficient power or knowledge to genuinely agree. We can be compliant out of laziness or fear, to avoid 'trouble', or to please someone else. Complicity is different and suggests a more active cooperation with knowledge of a possible wrongdoing. Both involve some form of consent, although this consent may not have been voluntarily given.

Some feminist literature works from the assumption that the power of men over women is such that women can neither consent nor dissent. This leads to the question of whether the relationship between women and men is one in which women can be active partners, passive victims or resistant survivors.

### No powerful women, please!

Power is currently defined in masculine terms, so I want to look at other ways of understanding it and achieving it. This requires more than just a reversal of roles and assumptions that what is male defined has to be wrong and vice versa.

The ability to exert influence is not necessarily about power in the sense of physical status. It is about the double-ended power relationship: the power that is both used and accepted. Power over someone involves its legitimisation by the less powerful. In its best sense, it is an acceptance by them that your ideas are based on deep knowledge, that your implementation is expert and you are in command of the situation.

Being trained to manage households, to rear children, to deal with the complexities of daily life was not designed as training in taking control. Yet in many ways women did manage all manner of spheres of control. In most cases they were running the household, even if some had little or no access to money. When men joined the wars women took over many of their jobs. There are numerous examples of women using power in public and private, even though their actions were not overtly identified by this word.

This mirrors the gender differentiated communities in non-industrialised and/or non-European societies which continue to allocate different types of power and spheres to women and men. While men are dominant in the public spheres women have defined other areas of power and influence.

So there has been, and continues to be, power and leadership amongst women. These are related and prescribed within a masculine elite set of definitions, but nevertheless offer a range of possible responses for women. These include compliance and resistance. Both options involve action, not just passive acceptance.

There is still a sense in which many fairly traditional women see they have power in the household, and even over what they regard as incompetent males. The 'Mere Male' column in

*Woman's Day* magazine recounts stories of male incompetence and is one of the indications of a powerful female ethos, albeit within a constrained framework. There have always been options for sanctioned power within an envelope of acceptability and expressed within feminine social culture. This is not the same for all women, as obviously race, class, culture and personal circumstances will affect the envelope and space women have.

The point to acknowledge, therefore, is that most women have some, if perhaps limited, power rather than being entirely powerless. From this recognition, increases in power can be seen as part of a progression rather than a radical shift to something completely different. We are not working in a vacuum nor are we seeking to reverse an entire power structure. What we need to do is move the sense of power women have into a broader, more public sphere and allow women to own it and use it in less familiar settings.

When women claim an extension of power and redefine its purposes and scope in ways that are unlimited by masculinist assumptions, it can be read as a positive achievement, not as a synonym for violence.

### Powerful woman!

This phrase is often used as a negative epithet to typify the power that men sometimes attribute to women. It encompasses particular male views of the power of our sexuality and may include the image of the dominatrix or the seducer. Often this power is defined as the power of the enchantress, the witch, the evil woman, who like Eve or Lilith entraps the powerless male.

This is attributed without the necessity for the women concerned to have any sense of their own power. There are some reflections of this in the discussion raised by men who argue that the images of violent and evil men, sometimes claimed to be promoted by feminists, do not reflect male feelings of personal impotence. However, these complaints do not recognise that the relative power positions of men and women in popular culture and media operate to the disadvantage of women by privileging men's images.

Helen Garner's tale *The First Stone*,[10] tells of possible sexual harassment in a university college, where two students lay complaints against the Master. She describes one of the young women complainants in glowing sexualised terms. At a public reading,[11] Garner was attacked for attributing power to the woman's appearance. She stated that she thought the young woman could not possibly see the Master of the College as powerful as he disempowered himself by kneeling to her.

Garner failed to see that the Master's presumed feelings and stance were irrelevant to the personal sense of power of the young woman. Her response was apparently to feel powerless, a victim to a male who was in a much more senior position with power over her. The book gave credence to a male-defined sense of disempowerment, which it valorised by describing perceptions of the woman's appearance, but the anger and pain which presumably were occasioned by the woman's sense of helplessness were disbelieved.

This debate illustrates the difference between a subjective sense of power and its gendered object within its social setting.

The body and sexuality of women are ascribed the power of robbing the male of his self-respect and control. Yet in this case it is the women who are accused of a misuse of power by reporting the case to the police.

There are men without much formal economic or institutional power, some with none. Some men create power within their peer groups in established male environments, like pubs or in workplaces. This was shown in the New Zealand film *Once Were Warriors*, where the leading male character's identity and sense of power were within the pub culture of drinking, parties and violence. Similarly, many women will not want power, or have restricted access to it because of class, race and other factors. These are issues of major concern but outside the direct scope of this book.

The interpersonal spaces in which Foucault locates power are, without doubt, important places for debate and resistance. While recognising that these are often the most immediate sites of power and problems, I have concentrated on larger institutions. I want to change these as a priority and they make very good examples of the way power is and is not misused. It is in these areas that we need to see the difference that can be made by the entry of many more women and the establishment of new directions and values.

These are the areas that regulate and distribute the resources of the community at large, which produce the mass media, which market the products and sanction wrongdoings as they define them. Without change at this level, the other sectors will still have these problems. Without changes at other levels, including the local and personal, the top-down changes will not be sustainable. So we need both, and much of what is written here will work at multiple sites, not just the ones I am directly addressing.

The ways of dealing with either small or larger organisations are not very different. Here we will be looking at power in governments; in lobby groups with influence; in religion; in producers of popular and high culture and media; in the community; and in big businesses and financial institutions.

A few women, allowed into such institutions on men's terms, sometimes enjoy a share of power and become part of the privileged minority. They are often isolated, forced into identification with male peers and/or are part of elite groups of women. They are entitled to be there and are often very useful but they work within the present models.

Some women working in these areas attempt to set up their own networks but these often focus on personal support. We cannot assume that they will be very different from the masculine ones since they are sanctioned in a largely male world. Women can change parts of the underlying male culture by being there and challenging some assumptions, and they often work to put more women in positions of influence. Generally however, their presence is only tolerated because these women are visibly succeeding on male terms and they would immediately become vulnerable if they threatened these substantially. Women are often also subject to considerable ridicule and male paranoia, particularly in organisations which are still largely male. These women are seen as a 'mafia' that threatens men's power.

## Can we have feminist authority?

Feminist authority is power women can sense, own and share. We can develop some alternatives to the present limited options. One type of power which is dealt with in the final section of this book is shared power. It involves moving away from the idea that there has to be one person at the top or that power and responsibilities cannot be shared.

I would like to propose that we add to discussions of power and leadership an expanded definition of what I will call authority. This is power as mutuality, sharing of obligations and responsibilities. It presumes the capacity, where necessary, to call on each other's knowledge and skills and to separate out some parts of the leadership role for solo action and others for joint action.

I want to signal ways in which power may be used that do not involve force and do not necessarily involve the very 'masculine' aspects of coercive or even individual power. The relative physical size of men and women has been a basis for allocating the attributes of power and force to men. What we need to look at are the power expert/authority attributes which need not be gender biased.

If we want models of power that are based on authority rather than strength we have to project conformity with, and confidence in, the ideas we hold. Therefore they have to be ones which are authentic for us. (In my thesaurus the term *legitimate* comes up in the entries for *authority* and *authentic*, and legitimacy comes from owning an issue.)

## Woman power

There have been some, but too few, occasions when I have felt a genuinely different kind of power. This is what I'd like to call woman power. Outlined briefly here are instances when I have been part of large assemblies of women with a common purpose, often openly feminist, and committed to making changes.

At the inaugural WEL (Women's Electoral Lobby) Conference in summer 1972, we overflowed Burgmann College, Canberra, when 600 of us turned up. For the first time ever, I was part of a mass of women who were working out what we wanted from a new Labor government. We believed, and so did the government, that women's votes had won them the election and we felt we would be listened to, and for some time we were. The process of deciding what we wanted and how we could achieve it was passionate and cooperative, and gave us a real sense of achievement, power and influence.

During the Mid Decade of Women United Nations Conference in Copenhagen in 1980, the official group—mainly men—was posturing in the hall, and there was a fight about whether Israel was racist in its policy on Arabs. Outside in the press area, I interviewed Leila Khaled on the problems of being a woman in the PLO. She was a former Palestinian activist who had been involved in an aeroplane hijack, and I am an ex-Jewish refugee. I liked her and agreed with much of what she said, and realised women could make odd connections outside the sanctioned male political power structure.

In 1982 at the Women and Arts Festival in Sydney, going

from concerts to art shows in the company of women, listening to other women, looking at what women had produced for other women, I felt for once, that we were in control.

In 1985, against all odds, women's organisations held a Women's Tax Summit in Canberra, six weeks before the National Tax Summit. Women's groups joined with welfare and consumer groups at the 'Men's' summit to produce alternative views which derailed the proposed consumption tax. We started a process that resulted in the defeat of the proposals for taxes which would have penalised low-income earners.

When I feel depressed by the problems I can identify and the still limited input we have, I remember those moments when groups of women came together and, against the odds, felt able to make small and large changes; when we felt our own power and worked in different ways.

Don't get me wrong, I am not romanticising what happens when women work together. Awareness of the problems women often create for other women, both in groups and individually, was one of the reasons I wrote this book.

### Health warning: Power is addictive!

There is no guarantee that women with power will not misuse it. We are as fallible as men, and as long as women leaders are few and usually selected by men, their input will be more limited than men's, and their individual failures seen as emblematic of the failings of women in general. It is risky to assume that women will wield power differently, particularly in the long term. In the short term, because women's life patterns are still different from men's, we are more aware of aspects of living and caring that they often overlook.

Many women want to use power within current circumscribed models. Some get pleasure out of 'playing the game'; others do it as a means to an end. Some men (and women) seriously believe that there should be no debate about power, as currently defined, and resist change because they argue it undermines 'natural' gender attributes and good order.

With the recent advent of the men's movement there are a number of men who feel that they too are oppressed by current gender assumptions. This debate has potential worth but at times seems disingenuous. During a radio discussion I had with two men who were putting piteous pleas for the plight of men, I suggested that if they were having such a terrible time then perhaps they could hand over some of their power to women.

No one with power gives it up easily, even if it is sometimes a burden, and they are equally reluctant to share it. This is not surprising; owning and using power is often very sexy, it creates excitement and feelings of elation and immunity to pain and failure, as well as the thrill that accompanies risk. These feelings can be quite intoxicating, with adrenalin and endorphins mimicking the highs of artificial drugs. Men ride these highs at Cabinet and board meetings or, more often, in the less formal settings where the deals are done. They are comfortable knowing their input will be effective, and are confident that they have the answers. It can be both scary and very attractive to those who aspire to share the spoils and benefit from the gains.

There is no easy answer to the seductiveness of power. We need to work out ways of using it, reframing it and, I hope, sharing it. We also need to engage in discussions about how we can change the concepts of leadership to make the solo and irresponsible highs less attractive.

# CHAPTER 2

## A Possible
## Feminist Future

There are particular changes I would like to see in the world, both globally and locally. Many women and men may well disagree with me, in the broad issues and in the details. However, I am not writing this book to convert you to my ideas, though it would be exciting if you were interested in exploring them further. Primarily, I hope to show that there is a variety of equally compelling views of how the world could be.

These views involve a fairer society, a more caring and creative culture, and do not allocate power and resources on gender lines. I would see these as feminist political theories. There are many other ways of constructing societies and economies, and elements in them are drawn from different belief systems and epistemologies.

Often I have heard people say that humans by nature are selfish and aggressive, and that we have to tempt people with money and not expect altruistic behaviour. When I ask these people whether this is true of themselves they deny it; it seems not all humans are greedy and self-interested, just other people. Yet this is the model of Economically Rational Man, who drives the equations in the economics that dominate public policy. The use of this term is one case where gender-excluding language is helpful as I can facetiously reply that men may be greedy by nature but women are not!

There are countless ways of looking at how the world works and of defining what constitutes society. Many are not the product of European male experiences. One example is that of Aboriginal Australian lore and practices which regard 'skin' relationships as powerful and binding, and by contrast the individualism of white cultures as brutal and shameful. We can look at this model to provide a starting point for changing the very individualistic cultures we brought to this country.

Do we know what a feminist future would be like? Can we design the world we want to live in, the one we want for our daughters and sons? If we recognise that the present dominant view is a certain and limited form of masculinism, we can then see that there are many more world views that we could realistically consider and others we haven't even dreamed of yet.

I do not just want women in positions of power. I wish to see women nominate the outcomes they expect to achieve. My hope is for explicitly feminist viewing points, rather than just woman-centred ones. What do I mean by feminist in this context? At its most basic, feminism is the political framework which seeks to remedy the unjust and inappropriate effects of the limited viewpoints of male dominance by incorporating the viewpoints of women. I am working from the premise that gender—that is, socially determined differences in expectations of men and women in all societies—means that women and men see the worlds we live in differently.

However, there is more to this issue than the identification of the dominant forms. Within a culture, subcultures comply, reinforce and, sometimes, contest the dominant forms. Those who benefit from the status quo will not work to change the culture. Therefore the subordinates have to deny the assumed legitimacy of the ruling elite, redefining both formal and informal structures and thereby bringing about change. To control what we want, women must move out of the position of the Other; from sometime critic to actualiser.

Women must define what we want, rather than complain about what we do not want. We need to move from being reactive to actively promoting alternatives. This means not focusing on the marginal, defined 'women's issues', but putting them in the context of what we want from the institutions as a whole. How do we want these institutions to change, not just to meet women's needs, but to serve the challenges of the contemporary world?

There is no one feminist answer any more than there is one economic answer. There are diverse views amongst those who call themselves feminists, and there are women who often support more traditional roles. What many of these viewpoints share is an awareness of the particular responsibilities allocated to women in most social systems and how these are affected by politicians and those who have power over us.

Women are expected to be carers and the managers of relationships. Some of us do this well, others less comfortably, some avoid it, but few of us fail to recognise what is assumed of us. By not taking account of women's points of view, public policy has effectively ignored the trade-offs between unpaid household services and paid ones. The development of alternative policy and social views by women, in particular those who would acknowledge their feminism, is apposite to an informed debate on possible futures. For this, there are many feminisms.

I heard Ann Oakley[1] on Sydney radio define feminism as a political view. On this same question, Rebecca West said that 'I myself have never been able to find out precisely what feminism is: I only know that people call me a feminist whenever I express sentiments which differentiate me from a doormat'.[2] This leaves space for us to fill.

### Restating the State

Starting at first principles, we need to look at the way we see the individual, the community and society. The basic unit in most western political theory is the rational individual. The view of the individual as paramount dates from the beginnings of the modern State and the industrial revolution. As the move from village to town, from home to factory occurred, there was a loss of tight community ties. Therefore, there was a perceived need for more governance: laws and processes to define the way people should behave. Political philosophers, trying to think through some of the massive changes that were occurring, invented the idea of apparently naked and solo men agreeing to give up their freedom to unite in a social contract.[3] This defined the social system as a collection of individuals agreeing to combine for mutual protection and advantage.

However, there was another aspect to this contract. It was

limited to those areas of public domain which were seen as appropriate for the rule of law, and excluded the private sphere of home and hearth. The modern State is thus founded on the differentiation between the female, still feudal household, and the public sphere of men.

Carole Pateman, a feminist political philosopher, reformulates this concept as the sexual contract.[4] This contract legitimises the public as the sphere of men and the private as the area outside the scope of the State. She sees this as a compact between men to exclude women from areas of power and influence, and proposes that the masculine bastion of the State may perhaps never be appropriately entered by women.

I am more optimistic and would like to put up another model. This looks at the way we connect in a very different manner to the one proposed above. I believe we can see ourselves, alternately, as starting life and civilisation as part of the tribe or group and as indivisibly linked to others in a web of community. There are those still living in tribal and feudal societies which emphasise people's interconnections and obligations to the larger group.

I am not romanticising a return to village and tribe. Connectedness is part of being human, but it is not all. Urbanisation offered an escape from what were often stifling social systems. Cities allowed the development of many new ideas, cultural activities and political groups. The individuals who could choose their associations often provided the processes of modern change.

For women, there were both gains and losses. The suffrage

movement—women's demands for recognition and rights—was a product of urban change. Access to education, to association with other women and with other groups were aspects of urbanisation. Jobs, even if they were bad jobs, were often seen to be better than housework or service in the home. The problem was that these jobs were in environments where women's needs were very rarely met or even considered.

This potted history recognises our joint needs for individual rights, mutual obligations and connections. We must develop social and political systems that integrate the home and family connections into a wider community setting as part of the main policy arena, not a side bar, incidental to the economy and everything else. If we start from this concept we can work with other definitions of human nature. If we challenge the assumption underpinning most of the dominant economic theories, that man (*sic*) is basically greedy and self-interested and therefore will always maximise his advantage, we can see that it is not the only way of conceptualising the world.

If, as I am proposing here, our sense of self is more related to our connections than to our wealth, we have to challenge current policy priorities. Although the needs we have for connections and belonging to a wider group are worth exploring at a personal level, they should also be on the public agenda. The private sphere has always acknowledged the connections; it seems the public area has been the problem. Women were always left with the care of others, so recognised mutual relationships were more important than individual greed.

Leaving so many of the private activities of women's roles

outside the realm of State regulation meant we were not citizens in the sense of free and equal recipients of the protection of the State. Now we have partially moved into the public sphere and we are dragging the household behind us.

Women's roles have changed: falling birthrates show that we can now take into our own hands what was once a biological imperative that had huge social consequences. The technological developments in housework and the changed nature of many of the tasks in the paid workforce require little or no dependency on physical attributes and so there are fewer gender differences in the capacity to perform lifting and heavy work, for instance.

Housework and paid work debates in the political sphere seem to assume that most women still give birth to five children and wash in a copper, and most men lift weighty goods on assembly lines. With these stereotypes becoming increasingly anachronistic, the diminishing physical demands on men and women in the workplace and the home should translate into greater possibilities of overlap in care and paid work responsibilities.

No such luck: the convergence has been accompanied by an increasing emotional role differentiation. This is the real issue that women face in late twentieth century, post-industrial society: the physical difference in tasks has been replaced by gender-defined roles in relationship managing and interpersonal responsibilities. This becomes an excuse for offering women the lower paid jobs and expecting us to retain primary responsibility for household and family management.

The problem is not only men avoiding household responsibilities, it is the design of the paid workplace which assumes that the workers do not have such responsibilities. In a feminist future we would need to redesign the workplace and the household to make it easier to move between the responsibilities of each and harder to use gender as the basis for allocating tasks.

We have to develop our own version of the future and decide how we want it to be. This could mean that we need to preserve what we have in common and value: the links that bind us and the sense of common wealth. We need to develop forms of social policy and leadership that value accepting responsibility for each other and for the future as first priority. We could develop some of the social policy areas in order to maintain and support a social system, rather than the individual and the family only.

We must recognise the importance of our sense of belonging in ways that don't exclude others or set up power hierarchies. The concept of world citizenship, the idea that social policy is care for a stranger,[5] or the adage that we should treat others as we would like to be treated, may seem old-fashioned but this doesn't mean they should be dismissed.

Seeing ourselves through relationships, I suspect, is one of our basic needs: as humans we see ourselves reflected through others and we identify our commonalities and our differences. We are creators of complex societies and cultures and we need to recognise the differences we derive from these cultures.

Lore, tradition and kin relationships work in small societies where direct contact between individuals is frequent enough to sustain familiar relationships. These do not guarantee care or generosity but need to be understood as powerful processes for the maintenance of traditional power and mutual obligations. However, the reality of big cities, immigration and moving away from families in mobile mass societies require us to take some responsibility for ourselves and others.

We need social theories to integrate the group and individual in an ongoing and healthy tension, where links and dissent are both validated. This would allow us to develop a singular ability to take ethical stances and argue for results we want to achieve. Only in validating this as a part of social structure can we hope to mediate and control the power for change we possess.

Therefore, we must bring in some of the best aspects of liberalism, the validation of dissent and the protection of individual rights, and mix them with obligations. This puts the responsibility on each of us to act ethically and protect others where necessary, otherwise we damage the group. Such a theory is untidy, but it fits the untidy world we inhabit, and which, no matter how hard we try, we never seem to be able to make orderly. This theory lacks the simplicity of markets or Marxism. It recognises and validates the complexity of human society and the need to create systems which can match our power to produce and destroy. Only by reflecting the tension between the individual and the group can we develop an understanding of the contradictions within which we operate.

This requires the ability to deal with ambiguity. It allows us to develop ways to move slowly towards a world in which we can all belong and share the resources. A world where we recognise the strengths of our ties to each other but at the same time remember that preservation of linkages does not translate to affirmation of the supremacy of the group.

Human beings are as capable of good as of evil, as able to absorb ideas of the virtues of altruism as of greed. What if we are tabula rasa, a clean slate, onto which the society inscribes its values? If we look at the ways in which societies define status, we can identify those in which status is gained more from giving than from owning. The Potlatch of North America and the Big Men of New Guinea are two examples where status is derived from giving to others, not by amassing one's own belongings.

The growth of the State during the last century was a sign that we were becoming more aware of the links that constituted society. There was, and always will be, a tension between what we want as individuals and what we want as people who are linked indivisibly to others. The balance swings but generally we seem to be in a meliorist society.

The past two centuries have presented us with major changes. We have moved from micro to mass societies and we have lost much of the sense of belonging that comes from knowing our links. This has been replaced by the links we vote for, appoint and establish as anchor points. The societies to which we belong have to be created by and with the common threads and by the provision of an inclusive set of institutions and services. We need new visions as the old ones no longer work.

### Shifting power, for all our sakes!

This book is not about doing over men, although often the public debate forces us into oppositional stances and assumes that women can only progress at the expense of men. It seems too hard for many people to differentiate between women taking on responsibility for a bigger share of decision making and women taking power away from men.

If we believed that power is limited to what is there now, this would be valid. In Part Three we look at alternatives which suggest that by sharing power, more of us can be involved. If we change the structure, the numbers will change too.

This can be illustrated simply by a recent meeting I addressed. A women's group were discussing the lack of women in senior community positions. One woman told of her role as the only woman on a board and of her welcome by the other five male board members. When I suggested the board should be half female, she said this was impossible as none of the men would stand down, so we suggested the board should be expanded to ten. This meant four more women could be appointed and four more sets of experience and ideas could be put to use in running the organisation. She found this too radical, but the idea added another dimension to the debate.

A few women at the top, and a few more on the way up, will not make a difference. They will be accommodated within the present system, and by paying someone to look after their children or households, they will insulate themselves against too strenuous an encounter with the other side of life. Even if they do care about these issues, the rules written by men will soon silence them, or reduce their influence. These are not the choices we want for women in leadership. Some will continue to go with what they see as the strength, the conventional 'wisdom'. They will support the present agenda, with a few deletions and additions if we're lucky.

What we need is more women at every level, enough to generate some solid debate about what should be on the agenda and where the priorities lie. These debates can also involve a diversity of male views, rather than just those of the elite few who are currently in power. However this is something men themselves need to tackle. As for our needs, the simplest major change would be for a range of women's views to be voiced.

This is radical without being destructive, as it is the single move which would substantially expand the range of experiences and attitudes of those in power. It would do this by representing the omitted experiences of over half the population. Also it allows a deepening, as well as a broadening, of knowledge on which decisions can be taken.

This is not an issue restricted to any one side of politics. Conservative and radical women have issues to raise. If this were to happen, the priorities and issues would no longer be gender biased. What we need after critical mass is achieved are the critical incidents; some spark, a radical move, a crisis or something which unites the group and can create serious shifts. The numbers are necessary but are not enough without the new ideas. I have offered my feminist future—there are many more out there, and we need to talk about them and develop them.

### Caveat emptor (Buyer beware)

This is a warning to you, the reader. There is always a pattern of change, both forward and backwards, good and bad. In outlining the case for more women as leaders, I have picked out the arguments that I hope will convince you. I tend to deal more with ideas than with feelings; this is one of the problems I sometimes have communicating with other women. I believe that we have to win on ideas as well as emotion because I have seen some of the problems emotion alone can bring.

This is an outsider's book and it had to be. If I had 'made it,' I would not be writing this material because those whom the club admits, lose their privileges if they criticise. The inside critics are few and the dilemma for us then becomes who to believe. Media contacts give me the power to make an impression from the outside; to offer insights as well as overviews.

Outsiders give a view of what happens with perspectives those inside do not and cannot offer. This is one of the reasons why feminism has been so powerful over the past two decades. It has provided a vantage point from which some of the injustices and idiocies that pass for social truths can be revealed.

# PART ONE

## CHAPTER 3

# Why Women are a Leadership Necessity

We need creative and broad-based solutions to the serious problems arising from the way the world is run. However, we are facing a dearth of good ideas and optimism about possible solutions to these global and national problems. A shift in the gender composition of leadership could well be a simple way to ensure the input of new ideas.

While this is not in itself any guarantee that the changes made will all be good, the viewpoints and experiences of women must extend the often very limited perspectives of the current incumbents. The diversification of input will provide at least a fertile ground for creative solutions and positive change.

This chapter looks at some aspects of the cultural and social climates in which we work, in order to describe the difficulties women have with being seen as leaders. It is not a description of formal barriers or institutional obstacle courses. The material here relates to the more subtle ways in which language, myths and images serve to make women very uncomfortable with recognising their leadership potential. The problem we have with conceptualising ourselves as leaders is only further evidence of the need for us to be there.

## In the beginning was the word (man)

I want to begin with the way myth and language confine us, as much of what I write will place readers outside their comfort zones. I will be mainly drawing on western traditions, though there are many similar examples from other cultures.

It was uphill all the way for women from the start of Judaeo-Christian traditions. In the beginning was the word and word was male. On re-reading the story of Creation, I found that Genesis provides a good example of the initial failure to recognise the leadership qualities of women. The story of Eve can be read as showing her leadership potential and a desire to make a difference. In search of knowledge she ate the forbidden fruit and induced Adam to follow her lead. It may not have been a wise decision but it initiated change. Yet God failed to recognise Adam's leadership inadequacies and both blamed Eve!

Hereby God failed the first application of the merit test because he continued to deal with the one (male) made in his own image. He used his power to reinforce the gender imbalances by legitimising Adam as having the authority to boss Eve. So, built into the story of the expulsions from the Garden of Eden is an early model of how women's leadership potential and skills were not only to be ignored, but cast as sinful and dangerous.

This account of Godly attitude is a powerful allegory for many women and men, and is still a barrier to promoting leadership as a female attribute as well as a male one. Many other myths have evolved from similarly gender biased beginnings, which meant that women had much early and bad press.

Another version of the 'women bring trouble' story is the Greek myth of Pandora's box. Again a woman could not resist temptation and opened the forbidden box, and was thus responsible for letting out all the woes of humanity. It is interesting and important to remember that the last thing out of the box, after all the woes, was Hope, who was a woman.

### Man power

The term *woman power* seems strange and unnatural. Power is seen as a male word, too often allied with force and violence. A discussion of female power usually relates to a perception of sexuality which entraps and enthrals men, and is seen as both dangerous and evil. In its political sense, power is the ability to do, to influence and to have an effect. It is intrinsically neither good nor bad; it depends on how it is used but it is often seen as corruptible and corrupting. It can be political or financial and these are areas usually associated with men. Power is also taken as a synonym for physical force which can be used to exact compliance and is again associated with masculinity.

Watch the television news, listen to the radio, flick through the magazines and papers. You will see and read about men doing what are considered to be men's things: playing football, going to gaol, having car accidents, and running most of the powerful institutions. Gangs, politicians, managing directors and top professionals generally have one characteristic in common; they are usually male. Why are the images of the extremes of power always male?

Think of a powerful woman. Can you? Try Boadicea, Maggie

Thatcher and stop a minute. Maybe Madonna fits here, but her power is different. Hers is not power gained through control of institutions, but the personal power of image manufacturing and success. Power as I'm interested in it here is the power over resources, not personal power.

Try to think of powerful men and the columns of figures stretch through time and space, the task is too big to manage. Why is power male? Just because man could swing the club at a sabre-toothed tiger eons ago and did not bear children, does this fit him to keep running the place now?

How did man get to be seen as the epitome of what was needed in power? Not all men are powerful, many are far from it and feel angry at being blamed for what is done by men in power. The men in power, however, have put their imprint on the image of power and leadership so absolutely that, to date, even women who 'made it' were often obliged to practise masculine leadership behaviour.

We are faced with the problem of defining ourselves in relation to the present structures. This means women must move in numbers into leadership roles to achieve even the possibility of change. Their presence and activity will then become a necessary prerequisite for correcting our myths and language traps so further and comfortable change may be possible.

## Difficult women and normal aggro men

The setting of gender appropriate behaviour is a serious issue. The assumptions about what is acceptable for men and women lead to some bizarre distortions and real problems for women who want to be leaders and men who perhaps ought not to be.

Part of the problem is the way women are selected for leadership. At present most are chosen by men or according to rules made by, and that serve, men. Thus we can imagine what happens to women who try to move into leadership positions and see why there are still so few. Start with images of women, of good women. Recognised womanly virtues still tend to be those of support and service in the domestic sphere, and there is a very limited allowance for public strength or visibility.

These are the messages that women take in from their earliest perceptions of the way the world works. Little girls are encouraged to make their mark in acceptable ways. They are not encouraged to promote themselves, but to wait for recognition. They are valued for their appearance, for their warmth, their empathy and goodness, all of which are passive.

Women are socialised to be supporters and helpmates, so it is often hard to reframe our identity as leaders. We tend to wait for men to start the process, to undervalue what we know, and slip comfortably into the secondary role. We don't volunteer but wait to be asked, and often, the shrinking violet waiting bashfully is trampled by a rushing male.

One of the fetters that hobble us is that women who are labelled as difficult are punished whilst others are rewarded for conformity and passivity. Difficult women are transgressors, to be excluded and often ignored until they learn their place and remember their manners.

This is a familiar process for me, as I was labelled difficult in many situations. I decided, not so long ago, that this was probably a badge of pride. Difficult seems to be a synonym for any activities that have change as an aim, or are seen to be feminist. This definition came to me after a series of personal and career problems which people explained away as being an outcome of my difficult personality.

On reading a few biographies of prominent women, I noticed a variety of statements basically saying the same thing, these were difficult women: Florence Nightingale, Beatrice Webb, Eleanor Roosevelt, for example. This started me wondering whether it was possible to find any woman who had made a difference in the public sphere who was not labelled difficult. Did the public view of women in English-speaking cultures define all activist women as difficult?

My questions on why it is so alien for women to lead multiplied, and the answers became even more alarming. If women are often not acceptable when powerfully and publicly advocating changes on their own behalf, it is even more difficult to see women as powerfully advocating changes for all.

There are women who adopt many masculine traits. There are groups of powerful women who play in the corporate areas whose circles are relatively closed. Increasingly they support other women so they can maintain their power roles, but they are constrained by their need or desire to conform so they can retain their positions or move up.

There are increasing networks of women in upper levels of organisations. These serve the function of allowing women, still rare in these areas, to meet. The women within such networks include chiefs of staff, women in management, women in the finance and superannuation areas, and so on. They provide mentoring and support and often see themselves as sharing many feminist goals, particularly the equitable treatment of women.

These are not 'difficult' women as by definition they must fit in. Some retain social and other links with feminist organisations and individuals, and play some significant roles in private. Many others have positions of power but eschew much contact with women of lesser power and status. A few of them recognise, actively or intuitively, that they will not be accepted in feminist circles as they have little interest in even supporting equity goals.

The growth of private-sector senior women's networks has obviously worked to promote some of the more acceptable issues onto the agendas of senior management. Corporate child care, equal opportunity strategies and similar measures are seen as enhancing the present system and are thus promoted. Given time other measures, aimed mainly at individual women, will be recognised as legitimate.

However, I have some concerns about how far these processes also militate against women who are 'different'. It is an interesting point to consider as it is possible that the very acceptability of these forms of feminism can reduce the acceptability of challenge, which leaves the proponents defined and excluded as difficult women.

The other side of the issue is that much of what is seen as normal male behaviour may itself be problematic. There are many studies of human behaviour which have been 'normed' on male subjects, leaving women able only to be labelled 'abnormal' or different. I want to illustrate the process with two stories which appeared one week in the newspapers. They show the gender biases which seep deep into our social and cultural souls.

The first article reported that a study of teachers' and children's assessment of which children were gifted, showed a class and gender bias towards boys. The ones children picked as talented were 73 per cent to 76 per cent male and 90 per cent middle class and 95 per cent Anglo. These assessments were shown to be clearly wrong by tests which measured talent and showed that talent was equal for boys and girls. The teachers thought boys were more likely to be talented because their behaviour matches our culture's masculine assumptions of what constitutes talent.[1] The findings of this study are particularly irrational as many other studies show girls being more compliant to school culture, and generally doing better than boys, who are more likely to be rebellious. This suggests teachers do not regard good work and behaviour as evidence of superior ability.

The second article covered a report by Dr Tony Jorm for the National Health and Medical Research Centre on male mental health.[2] Dr Jorm looked at what had been defined as normal male behaviour. To quote:

*Many typically male behaviours which had previously been seen as normal have been re-assessed and are now classified as symptoms of medical disorder. A decade ago most surveys, both here and overseas, did not include things like reckless, aggressive antisocial behaviour, or drug and alcohol abuse, all of which are now recognised as expressions of mental disorder.*

Dr Jorm goes on to say, 'In childhood, boys have double the

prevalence of mental health disturbance because they externalise their problems usually with aggressive, antisocial or under-controlled behaviour'. The study showed that during adolescence, girls catch up by internalising their problems and reacting with anxious and over-controlled behaviour. This leads to 'female' symptoms such as depression or being seen as deviant. However, problems experienced by boys, such as aggression, are assumed to be normal male behaviour rather than alternate expressions of mental disorder.

These are just a couple of indications of the way certain types of antisocial behaviour can be legitimatised because they form part of a ruling culture. If behaviour is a continuum, there is a risk that we see behaviours which are essentially antisocial as being acceptable.

It is important to recognise these gender norms and male values as they go far beyond conventional debates about including women in decision-making processes. If masculinity defines normality, often by aggression, competition and fear of closeness, this has serious implications for all our futures. These manifestations may put us at risk and cause serious problems in both the institutions that run so much of our lives and their leadership models.

In extreme cases, there are also more group-centred forms of aggression, such as cults, fundamentalist religion, football hooligans, gangs, ethnic revolts, and other manifestations of insecurity about the future. Here people trade their individual responsibilities to belong to a group which provides them with identity, justifications for existence and protection.

Some extremist groups tend to follow very masculine models of behaviour with aggression and violence being built into the process. Women are usually involved as hangers on and it is interesting to note that relatively few women have ever chosen to develop their own cults. Female gurus are rare and tend to use less aggressive controls.

## Tall poppies and squashed weeds

I have been threatening for years to offer an alternative to the many optimistic biographies of women role models, such as the *Tall Poppies* series. I am not criticising those books, it is important to record our foremothers and current achievers. My companion version was to be called *Squashed Weeds* and would tell the stories of those of us who have tried, but have not been deemed successful by the standards of male defined worlds.

I am concerned that the promotion of successful women is not balanced by recognition or analysis of the structural problems many women have faced and are still facing. There is a danger that the successes and failures are seen to be due to individual efforts and faults instead of system failures. In part, the optimistic views have been deliberately used by many committed feminists to present positives and not dwell discouragingly on the problems. The upshot has been that there is little public acknowledgment of the hidden problems in the cultures of organisations, such as who talks to whom, where information goes, who is hushed and what is ignored. These are often much more powerful than the visible and formal discriminatory structures, and the problems they cause are not described and not addressed. This has resulted in many highly competent and creative women being sidelined in innumerable small and major moves.

Amongst the casualties there have been many women whose ideas deserved a better hearing than they received and whose skills were often grossly undervalued. We need to determine what continues to go wrong so we can try again without the patterns being repeated. This is not easy because many of the women who have 'failed' assume they were at fault. Their sense of inadequacy is reinforced by the double standards set for women and men in senior positions. For example, criticisms of personal styles and interpersonal skills are applied to senior women in ways they are never applied to men. Hidden dress codes mean that colleagues may give undue attention to the colours and styles of a woman's clothing. Also, assumptions are made about women's emotional states, family responsibilities and other aspects of what are seen as female roles. Most relevant here is the difference in assumptions about core roles and skills, which means that women as change agents are particularly likely to be deemed unfeminine. Pushing 'women's interests', even if this is in a woman's job brief, may easily be seen as biased or unreasonable.

When women are asked to participate in public life, it is often to represent the areas they are seen as expert in. We have been successful in the last few years in establishing 'women's issues' as important. Now no political party would go to an election without policies on these issues and having a spokeswoman on women. (I would challenge this categorisation though; the issues are more than women's ones, and the idea of all women sharing one interest and spokesperson is absurd.)

However, even if it is in her job description, the person is further hampered by having to promote women's interests in an appropriately polite and compliant way. She must avoid being seen as too feminist or strident, and certainly not appear too powerful or ambitious. This presents women with real problems as power is the ability to make things happen.

Yet it is assumed so often that failure of women in senior ranks is their own doing. There are no interviews, surveys or case studies I can draw on for data here but my own observations. Few of the women who have been damaged want to discuss publicly the problems they have met. Those still working in the major institutions are often silenced or don't want to be seen as critical; others may have moved on and do not want to revisit what happened.

I don't want to produce a book of failures as this would only serve to discourage others. The victim model (poor us, we were done over) is likely to act as a deterrent to future involvement, which is the last thing I want. I maintain that women should not escape the responsibility of being part of the big decisions which affect us.

This is not an either/or situation. We need to work at a multiplicity of levels, which was the basis of the strategies we developed in the 1970s. Despite some claims of younger feminists that the women in the second wave were only concerned about equality, we were not interested in simply sharing what men had, but in changing the world by our presence.

## Add women, then stir

Many influential women are faced with the question of whether or not they should continue to do battle. Most of them have not had much success in changing the content of the decisions made, and we should not have expected them to do so. Their loyalty and contracts are with those benefiting by the present system and they usually made it into senior ranks by paying their dues.

Some women have managed to initiate some change and this needs to be noted and feted. Others serve who also stand and wait because by being there they change the visual and aural images of the organisations—women are seen to be involved. However, in looking at why women need to be in senior positions, even if not visibly making changes, the old recipes of second-wave feminism still work. If we read books about almost anything written prior to the 1970s, few mention women at all. History books, political texts, sociologies of communities and other purported objective descriptions and analyses often ignored women and assumed that men were the norm. Post 1970s, this changed somewhat with most books on general and social issues including separate chapters on women.

This recipe ensured that women were covered but still isolated in a separate section, giving the impression that society's standards were set by men and that women were a minority. We can also see the results of books which are now set reading for Women's Studies courses. These have their own sections even in relatively conservative bookshops, but still leave the other areas of politics and economics, for instance, relatively free of women's input.

So the entry of women into print is moving slowly towards a more reasonable coverage of women as authors and women as subject matter in the non-fiction areas. The next stage must be to incorporate feminist discourses across the board and not just under the heading 'Women's Studies'.

This process is a metaphor for other forms of progress: women need to be visible and to indicate their minority status as a precondition for further change. The lesson is that it is necessary to have had the separate 'chapters' so we can move on to whole books; women holding some power is chapter one of a process which still has far to go.

I have observed that the absence of women is rarely noted in a group or organisation. Men are used to an all-male universe, especially in senior or exclusive groups and only the entry of a woman makes the gender disparities obvious. The ability of one woman to influence or change decisions in any such situation will be extremely restricted. Even if she wished to have a significant input, her chances are very limited. I have no doubt that some women on boards, where they are often only one or occasionally two, undertake major efforts to make changes. However, they are reminded that their roles are to represent all constituents, and raising women's concerns is often seen as special pleading.

We need to reduce the quite unrealistic expectations on the few isolated women who are in senior positions, doing what they can. They generally owe their position to men because they were selected by men, supported by men and are surrounded by them. With a few notable exceptions, they have had little impact on changing the culture of leadership.

Setting up the change process as a battle which allows women to be seen as aggressive, or even worse as aggressors, is one of the best ways of alienating other women. Many women in senior positions have to choose their issues to survive in often hostile, or at least, alien environments.

### Creating a climate for change

Change is neither necessarily good or bad. The development of modern societies has produced both gains and losses. The interpretation of the benefits of change is subjective and a factor of your position within the social system. Having employment and decent living standards (or no job and little money), feeling as though you belong (or like an alien), enjoying the new (or preferring the wilderness), are just a few examples of how change affects us individually or in categories.

Changes in the gender balance are particularly problematic because the shift is sometimes within a very small space. The household/family usually contains both men and women and changes here are as much part of the process as shifts in the membership of parliaments. Creating a climate in which this change is seen as potentially positive is not easy. Some men believe that women's gain is their loss, others just find the concept of more egalitarian relationships unattractive. Some women also do not necessarily welcome change as they prefer the familiar structures of the status quo.

Therefore 'selling' the advantages of change requires access to media which are both sympathetic and interested in reform. This is an issue that is canvassed in many other publications, particularly in equal opportunity texts, so I do not intend to detail the problems women face with stereotyping, lack of representation and sexualisation of images. These are issues for the women's movement in general and present a constant set of problems.

However, the ridicule of feminist initiatives under the term *political correctness* is one aspect of the image process that I want to look at. This is a form of ridicule often applied by conservatives to language changes and gives many media people cheap laughs. It makes women very wary of being identified with feminism generally and feeds into an image of humourlessness and pettiness. This makes it one of the most difficult aspects to deal with.

Think about when the term is used. Apart from the wannabefunnies who twist their intestines at the humour of 'personholes', the main users are the populist power brokers who employ the term to send up any attempt to undermine the powerful. There are no examples of people using it for any streams of thought or terms which come from those who support the status quo.

The epithet 'political correctness' is often hurled at me by a range of media commentators and failed comedians. This irritates me intensely because there is a naivete about many users who feel they are protecting free speech rather than inhibiting it.

I find it fascinating that a few cases of over-the-top reformist zeal have received worldwide notoriety as examples of political correctness gone haywire. In this group we can put the Antioch College dating rules and the UK school principal who prevented students attending *Romeo and Juliet*. I am not concerned here with the rights and wrongs of these examples but do want to point out how widely and well the stories travelled, like urban myths. The issue is that these two minor examples are always quoted.

There are no equivalent radical examples which act as a unifying banner for many of the groups who are accused of PC. These are often the least powerful groups in the community: women, people from non-dominant cultures and people with disabilities.

The main problem is that there is a malign and deliberate attempt to use the phrase to actually kill off free speech and dissent, not to promote it as some may claim. By constantly harping on the phrase, commentators create self-censorship and anxiety in women who are speaking on behalf of other women. Yet what is spoofed as politically correct are generally the anti-establishment rules, and thus the spoofing acts as a form of social control on behalf of the status quo. The term is almost always used by the populists and powerful to suppress dissident voices. It stops people saying they are pained by certain words, it embarrasses people into silence. In the western world it claims to be about free speech but it is generally about majority domination.

I want to reverse the tables briefly and expose the continuous pressure on us all to conform to real social and political correctness. This is the almost invisible but pervasive range of ideas and wisdom which is so often and clearly disseminated that we can fail to realise how ideologically biased it is. Debates on women's right to 'choose' to stay at home with children, to 'choose' to be supported, are very 'correct'; that is, not to be questioned but not referred to as PC. On the other end 'competition' is seen as correct but no economist is accused of PC when they claim it's good for us.

## Excuse me, your values must be showing!

We are all ideological; that is, we have beliefs and values which we use to understand our worlds. Some of these are articulated as a complete system by political movements and religions so we have a total framework to use, but most of us muddle along with bowerbird mixes of experience and beliefs.

These frameworks can be shifted and the changes are transmitted through people and media in a multitude of ways which may be subliminal. We often think that what we believe is real and is the only way to see the world. To make changes then, we need to shift this understanding. If we believe that the world can't be changed without ruining what we already have, we tend to support the status quo. This is partly why those who advocate changes that threaten current privileges have many difficulties in being heard. We rarely have access to mainstream media on an ongoing basis; we come from outside and, at best, become regular guests on other people's programs. The mainstream concerns are regarded as somehow legitimate, as are attacks from more conservative views, but radical views are not seen as needing serious attention.

However, those radical views are considered to be good

subjects for ridicule, for undercutting in humorous ways, and of being in need of 'balance'. The mainstream and conservative views that control the debates are never seen as policing the system because they own it. In an almost ridiculous contradiction, efforts for change are believed to be an attempt to take control rather than a challenge to existing implicit control.

One of the more difficult tasks I have when talking to groups about change is creating confidence that there are other ways of moving on than those presently on show. This is the direct consequence of the suppression of genuine debates over the last few years. It seems to have led to a sense of futility amongst many who see no point in seeking change.

We tend not to act if we lack the vision or sense of what is possible, if we feel that our efforts are ineffective and it is all too hard. Taken to its extreme, this sense of powerlessness can also lead some people into some fairly nasty forms of self protection. These may be individual, like alarms on houses, increased gun ownership, high walls and isolation in fear of others, or may be groups like private, walled communities.

One problem we face, as members of the non-dominant group, is that we are better critics than future strategists. As change needs direction, women not only have to move to senior positions but offer direction for reform; let's start thinking about small changes and then move to bigger ones.

### Leading edge changes

In writing this book I am conscious that it will be read by individuals, and so I range between what you can do by yourself and what we need to do in concert. The problems we face are not individual ones and the opposition we meet is most often at the level of institutions. These include governments, businesses, and communities that have their own rules and ways of managing formal and informal structures which largely reflect hierarchical command systems.

This suggests that it is imperative to change the institutions. There is a growing, but still limited, recognition that the formats of the major organisations have been designed by and for men, powerful men. They have built into the functions and culture of organisations the defence mechanisms to sustain them past the particular generation of the men who set them up.

Looking for explanations of the process of change sent me back to Max Weber who, at the end of last century, was one of the first to look at how bureaucracies work.[3] He examined how an archetypical bureaucracy, the then Prussian Civil Service, resisted modernisation.

He suggested that institutions, such as governments and the Church, have as a first law their own survival. Their response to threats of change is to co-opt the change agents, absorb them, and thereby defeat them. A century before, another man, William Godwin, who's now better known as Mary Wollstonecraft's husband, theorised that anything that becomes institutionalised ossifies. This was an extraordinary insight given that it was made so long ago, at the beginning of so many institutions. It was the time of the French Revolution, the founding of the USA and European settlement of Australia, when little of what we have since invented for governments even existed.

Both these philosophers recognised that the structures set up by those in power develop a 'life' of their own. This creates difficulties as the selection of successors to positions of power is made on the basis that they will serve the institution. The evidence over the past century has shown the extraordinary ability of systems to self-repair and survive.

People who run institutions react from fear of change itself, as well as fear of losing some of the large and small privileges that they currently have. They support what they have because it is familiar and, particularly for the rank and file at the lower, less powerful levels, what comes next may be worse.

The task of making real changes that involve the alteration of existing power relationships in government, business and other institutions is going to be hard. For women to make significant structural reforms will involve taking some power from men, and thus reducing the influence of the present cultures of masculinity which have become self-sustaining.

I am not positing a conspiracy theory to explain why change is so difficult. There are no committees of men meeting on Monday mornings to work out how to make women's lives harder. If this were true we would have to assume that individuals are more rational and ordered than we usually are. It also ignores the culture of organisations and structures set up to resist change. Of course, there are those who are well served by the status quo who will reinforce the existing defences, but often the main problem is that those storming the barricades fail to aim for the weak spots.

Some ideas for changing the guardians, for replacing a significant proportion of the current power brokers with new faces and new ideas, are proposed in the last part of the book. This section is confined to pointing out that this is a necessary and urgent task.

## CHAPTER 4

# What We Need to do
# to Make Our Way Up

If Norm is male and Adam was a rough draft, can men do it without our input?

In this chapter I look at the areas in which men predominate, such as government and business, and at decision-making processes. The following material makes a case for ensuring that the present masculine culture which dominates society is restructured before it does any more serious damage.

The year 2000 hovers in the near future and polls and reports show that more than ever there is a sense of anxiety in the community. The questions being asked relate to a feeling of disquiet with the directions, not just from women, but throughout society. A Newspoll international barometer of twelve countries[1] showed Australia as one of the countries most worried about issues like employment, living standards, the environment, violence, and also one of the most concerned about inequality.

There are few signs that any of our usual countries of comparison are feeling good about the future. The USA is having serious problems with internal terrorism and there is huge dissatisfaction with government. The UK is experiencing problems too as it battles a slow decline and loss of social cohesion. Inequalities are rising in most developed countries and there seems always to be a war on somewhere.

The ideas of the left and the old paternalistic conservatism have both been discredited. Until now there had been some balance kept between the two superpower systems with different views, but with the collapse of communism, dominant thought has become even narrower.

Leaders of government, business and the community are not finding easy answers, and there is a lack of confidence in their expertise. There is a strong growth in fundamentalism and ethnic, religious or ideological cults which offer a very simple solution: believe us and obey, and you will be saved.

These problems are the result of what were presumably the best efforts of primarily male leaders, or the occasional woman, like Thatcher, running on the models developed by her male peers. So we can see there is a need for different leaders who can bring in new ideas and make them work.

The following material looks at what we face in a world defined largely by and for men, and raises serious issues of distorted perceptions and unfair representation. These limits come from the interests and perceptions of masculinity. Let me make this clear: I am referring to the problem of a form of normative masculinity, not men, which entraps not only women but men whose values are different and who themselves experience different cultures and needs. By this I mean that there are characteristics imposed on men so they are trapped into being 'normal' and not allowed to deviate. This dominant masculinity puts a high value on competition, aggression and self-interest which requires almost complete absence of the social and communal. This belief system underpins public policies and economics. For example, look at the ways in which individual, masculine-approved power behaviour often mirrors the major actions of international business and politics.

I use the term *masculine* deliberately, not as another term for patriarchy or male dominance, even though it may be a by-product. It describes the limits of perception that have affected the ruling (male) elites of western European capitalism. Their fixation on market dogma and exclusion of women from decisions in the public realm have always been a problem, but have reached unparalleled dominance through a particular confluence of money markets, increasing isolation of elites and technological speed of decision making. When domestic need and chores, nurturing, child rearing and everyday life are physically separated from paid work and power, the current problems multiply.

## Man-aging government

I am concerned here with the different manifestations of the gender biases in the system, particularly within governments. A very obvious one is the priority given to certain types of spending and policy making over others. If we can say that the roles and functions of governments are gendered, then the areas deemed as male—defence, economics, trade, mining, agriculture and industry—have always been seen as serious and important. Other areas, such as education, welfare, health, the social wage and service areas, are considered secondary and spending in these areas must not threaten the areas listed above.

These different priorities started the process of creating an artificial division between what was done in the home (nurturing and unpaid household production), and the world of traded labour and goods, which was the legitimate sphere of economy and government. Most of the areas left to women were shut out of the public arena. A major complaint from women over the past decade is that much of what we do in the home and community is unpaid and is not recognised as work or as part of the economy. It is not counted in the Gross Domestic Product (GDP) so officially it does not exist.

This, coupled with a particular set of precepts, made it possible for western civilisation to develop its modernist pressures for progress. These stressed a model of individualism which fitted into a society based on contract, on urban living and industrial and colonial enterprises. Men progressed by competition and self-interest and women were an attachment, left at home to provide unpaid services and comfort.

As the State expanded during the nineteenth century, education, care of children, health services and other responsibilities previously managed within the household were picked up by government. Also, much of the household production moved into mass-production for sale. So the paid sectors of production and services paralleled many aspects of those of the household.[2]

This was the public/private split which has continued to the present. For a long time, we have expected more and more services to move from the household into the paid sector. The last two decades, however, have seen a contraction of both government spending and expectations of what the taxpayer should or would provide.

Where once children were educated at home and most health care was home based, these have become public services. However, the move towards day surgery and de-institutionalisation, no matter how well intentioned, usually ends up cutting costs and puts the responsibility of care back onto the household. The uncosted community sectors have always allowed State and commerce to rely on an unwaged, unprotected, home-based system that supported the public sphere.

The role of government is more concerned with macho competitiveness and less concerned with the provision and regulation of services. The so called 'level playing field' echoes the male imagery which sees life in terms of economics with wealth creation as the goal. The family then becomes the unpaid replacement for what markets do not provide.

### Tipping (women in and men out)

Over the past two decades we have watched the development of an interesting contradiction. The governments that accepted the precepts of Reagan and Thatcher have become more aggressively concerned with masculine priorities, at the same time as feminism put some feminised issues on the agenda. Issues such as domestic violence, child care and equal pay involved more government intervention and resources and resulted in some previously private issues being moved into the public sphere.

Reductions in government spending took place at the same time as the special pleadings of disadvantaged groups were heard. The Australian version of this was tagged as social justice, with the objective being to allocate the diminishing resources to those who could prove most needy. This gave rise to what I dubbed 'competing victim syndrome', where all outgroups sought to prove that their disadvantages qualified them for more of the limited public purse.

In my more paranoid moments, I wonder if it is a coincidence that as soon as women demanded that more issues concerning them went onto the public agenda, men started reducing the legitimacy of the government spending. This situation developed in the mid 1970s in Australia. The 1980s saw the strange contradiction of reduced funding as a proportion of GDP for government overall, but increased funding going to services such as child care and refuges. What this meant was that we were receiving an increasing amount of an ever diminishing cake.

We did not predict the major change in the perception of the legitimacy of State activities and intervention. By 1974, the reform agendas of the 1960s were under threat due to some major shifts in the international finance markets with the Arab oil shocks and the slowdown of postwar growth in western industrialised nations. Instead of new claimants on the State being accommodated by growth, and therefore not threatening existing distributions, limited growth created a tax revolt and the ascendancy of monetarism. The non-interventionist State became the ideal of most English-speaking countries.

The rhetoric of market forces qua economic rationalism was alien to the framework pushed by the 1970s feminists. We naively thought the mixed economies with ever-increasing State activities were a given, and our arguments about justice and liberation would be heard. The last two decades have seen some of the social problems that feminists identified move from the private sphere to the public: domestic violence, incest and rape have generated costs in legal and support services; child care, care for the aged, increased community services for families and domiciliary supports are demanded as fewer women and communities pick up unpaid work; equal opportunity and anti-discrimination programs are supported and funded by governments. Although this movement from household to paid service has been productive in these instances, many of the services that have been generated are seen as bandaids, are funded reluctantly and relatively cheaply, and often exist under the constant threat of cuts.

In this process we created an agenda for women. The issues we raised have been defined as women's issues and marginalised from the major debate. So although we were successful in most countries in re-routing funds into feminist-raised issues, we did so without affecting the mainstream agenda. By maintaining that these were women's issues and having them dealt with by women's ministers and femocrats, they remained quarantined from the 'real' role of the State. This leaves them vulnerable to political shifts to the right and of definably less important status than economic issues.

A serious threat is now appearing as many of the concerns raised under the category of women's issues are being moved into the category of gender issues and even into men's issues. This is happening in education, for example, where girls' programs are now gender programs and refocused on boys. This does not, unfortunately, mean that these concerns are accepted as mainstream problems, as genuine critiques of a system that serves neither women nor men adequately. Instead, angry men, ill served by mainstream machismo, are demanding their share of women's small equity resources.

There are other areas where issues have been moved into the mainstream, such as child care. However, even here there is still an undercurrent of illegitimacy as recognition of the importance of funding of public child care fluctuates in and out of favour. Our success in Australia has not been matched in the USA or UK where child care is still regarded as a private issue. Even here it is always seen as a possible savings option in the budget run-up. If women remain the main carers, this will continue to be one problem that men will never have to understand.

In the last decade there has been a range of small gains for women against an overall trend which has seen serious losses in both rhetoric and dollars. Market forces and competition are now validated as major distributors of goods and services, with the public sector being reduced to a wide mesh safety net.

There is now much writing on the 'new' roles of governments and the public sphere which focus on reducing intervention and increasing the use of markets. This raises interesting issues for feminists because it was the government and public spheres that offered women the best options for services and support, as our lack of access to money made open markets inaccessible.

At the beginning of the current wave of feminism we believed that we were going to make serious changes to the system. While I acknowledge the possible naivete of our optimism, we were working towards what we saw as feminist futures. By joining the system we believed we could change it, unaware of the difficulties and resistance we would encounter. So the clarity of hindsight needs to be tempered with an acknowledgment of the optimism we had then for the possibilities of change.

We need active women participating in the State, able to pursue a reform agenda that does not put a heavy burden back on women in the unpaid sector. With an aging population and falling birthrate, it is necessary to use some forms of communal provision which cannot be left to markets and will not be controlled by men who have no responsibilities in the home.

### Man-aging a workplace

Men made workplaces in their own image. This does not mean all men enjoy their paid work, nor that all workplaces are uncomfortable for women. However, it suggests that the process which removed production work from the household into factories assumed that the workplace commanded the full attention and commitment of its workers. This meant in practice that there was little acknowledgment of the workers' outside roles, as parents and citizens for example.

The assumption, often implicit and still extant, was that one arrived at work clothed, fed and washed and therefore had no concerns about the exigencies of daily life. The workplace could take over your sense of self, and become the source of community and identity. This separation from the home made the workplace very masculine, largely male populated and left the home to women.

Even when women were employed, there was little recognition of the double role most carried. Women employees were expected to be as free as men of the chores of everyday life. While there are now shorter hours, and the recognition that there is more to life than paid jobs, there is still the expectation that women's role is to deal with the family and manage the personal relationships.

This affects the way management skills are defined. The new managerial and leadership criteria start from masculine norms and move very slowly to incorporate some feminine character-istics. Over the past decade, remedial training has been used to change certain less desirable masculine behaviours into more feminised skills, such as in the area of communication. But men still set the standards and women are expected to follow them.

Without a level playing field or racetrack, to mix some met-aphors, we play the potholes while the other side just moves the goal posts. This makes a nonsense of both our input and its effect as the metaphor should not be a game with winners and losers, but a productive process of cooperative enterprise.

There is widespread recognition that management on old lines is in trouble. A *Financial Review* article[3] quotes a Professor Lawler from the USCA's business school, who says the old Taylorist models based on dividing tasks and roles is finished. Lawler calls for major changes in both form and content of management: increased self-management, more generalist workers and more group involvement. These suggest models of the workplace more akin to households and community associations than to the traditional divisions of labour on the industrial production line.

There are also concerns and debates on the quality of management education and the need for better outcomes. A major supplement on management education[4] raised many of the problems facing Australian managers. In 1991, Australia had 770 000 business managers, of which only half had any formal training. Presumably the others learned on the job, and all, hopefully, through life experience. The problem is that this so-called life experience is generally limited to the workplace where the managers are surrounded primarily by other men with similar experiences.

In 1993, Australia was ranked twelfth on a scale of competitiveness but seventeenth on the management scale in the same study, which is an indicator that we have some problems.[5] David Karpin of CRA, head of the Commonwealth Government's inquiry into management education (The Industry Taskforce on Leadership and Management), identified gender as an issue. In an interview for the *Financial Review* he stated:

*As for women and management, we may have gone backwards in the last ten years, at least at the senior level. That is not just an equity issue—the majority of consumer decisions are made by women and a woman's perspective is important from the shop floor to the boardroom. What companies have to do is give women a chance to succeed or fail, otherwise they cannot prove their merit.[6]*

While some might cavil with the idea of 'a women's perspective', rather than a variety of perspectives from women as well as men, Karpin's recognition is an indication that the lack of women is an issue of efficiency, not just equity. Although I agree with him on this point I do have some concerns at his failure to question whether the merits on which women (and men) are judged are those appropriate to a changing work environment. If, as the article suggests, 85 per cent of training is on the job, the relative role of formal education is small. So I would suggest that the types of informal learning women and some men bring from the family and community should be included in the recognised skill base of managers. Adding to these formally does not necessarily mean that either men or women in senior ranks will question the dysfunctional aspects of senior masculine executive culture.

Many women in senior management or on boards do not see the cultures within which they work as needing to be changed. At a conference on women, power and politics,[7] some senior women indicated their personal rejection of male structures but paradoxically failed to question the legitimacy of the structures themselves.

An example of this was a paper by Helen Lynch who had resigned from her very senior job at Westpac Bank. She criticised the way big businesses are run and also offered serious criticisms of the failure of the private sector to use women's skills. She outlined the risks this raises for business in going for conformity and not the diversity and divergent thinking women could bring. However, she stopped well short of a more general critique of the damage that current masculine models have already imposed on big business. She sees change as building on what is, but like many other women, feels alienated enough to look for alternatives. Many women choose to go into their own businesses or work as consultants, seeing the problem as their own inability to put up with the slow change.

Margaret Jackson is one of the few women who have been admitted to multiple boardrooms, including BHP. Interviewed on ABC radio about her role, she saw nothing odd in the demands made on her time at senior level, nor for the need to place primacy on the workplace above all else. She saw this as a choice that people wanting the responsibilities at senior levels had to make. Even questions from the interviewer, Geraldine Doogue, raised no doubts about the excessive time demands.

These examples illustrate how rarely the adequacy of the model of senior management is questioned per se. Few seem to see that present structures may be seriously or even fatally flawed by their own criteria. Either they regard them as a matter of choice, one they would argue that women can make as easily as men, or as changing but too slowly. The problem as I understand it is that there are serious limits in the decision makers' experiences that make it extremely difficult for them to objectively assess their options.

The time question alone raises serious issues of workplace competence. The hours worked per week by men in senior management positions has risen dramatically during the past decade, with most going over the top of the Australian Bureau of Statistics scale, working fifty plus hours.[8] These hours allow little or no time for other activities and cast serious doubt on the efficiency and effectiveness of the worker. We do not let pilots, truck drivers or bus drivers work long shifts because tiredness reduces their capability. I cannot see why it should be any different for those who purport to run the country and its major businesses. How can regularly working fifteen-hour stints, and more, make any sense? In fact, it may in part explain some of the problems we are facing.

A serious and structural problem raised by this corporate, high-flier lifestyle and the gender of most of those involved in it, is that it denies people time for any form of participation in family and community life, let alone contact with the wider world. This suggests that the characteristics necessary for entry onto boards and senior management include certain levels of obedience to corporate structures and the sublimation of one's personal life, which might not be the best traits for good decision making. The *Australian Financial Review* editorial on International Women's Day 1995, suggested that the hungry, aggressive characteristics needed to make it in the business environment may not actually be necessary for the tasks involved.

Our own experiences affect our judgment. A world almost always confined to offices, boardrooms, airport lounges and planes is not one conducive to making good assessments of anything. Look at the lifestyles of senior staff. Most senior men are excused from shopping, housework, taking the children to school, or dealing with a sick child and the exigencies of the health-care system. They rarely have contact with the public-transport system, make their own family and friendship maintenance calls, cook or arrange a meal. After all, they are excused everyday living as they have the world to run. But which world is it exactly that they are running? This is not universal, though the exceptions are too few to make a difference.

It is interesting to look at what happens to men working in traditionally female occupations. A recent study, by Claire Brown from Southern Cross University,[9] of nursing in New South Wales showed that while men made up only 8 per cent of registered nurses, they already held more than 20 per cent of the most senior positions. Although this is usually attributed to men working full time for longer periods, Brown's study showed men were also often promoted after relatively short times in their jobs.

This study and others[10] found that male nurses were highly conscious of their masculinity, because they were valued for being physically more able. They also thought they were caring but some felt they lacked the intimacy of women's forms of care. This indicates that men may feel that they have to be more virile in their jobs to avoid losing their appropriate gender power roles. In turn, this may lead them to seek promotion and display leadership traits in more visible ways than their female peers. As well as finding comfortable working relationships with senior male medicos, this means they are more likely to be seen as management material.

This suggests that even feminised areas of work have been unable to leave any long-term alternative imprint. This is probably because hospital management has always remained primarily male and dominated by medical models, in which the management are not medically qualified. A management structure in health care in which Chief Executive

Officers (CEOs) are the administrators, still follows very masculine models. Also, the employment of men in the feminised area of nursing allows senior men to deal with other men, further reducing female influence.

## Man-aging decisions

The lifestyle of senior managers in the public and private sector is not only a problem for the individual but also for the communities affected by the decisions taken. In Australia we have a perfect illustration of this in the unreal atmosphere of our national capital, Canberra. It is not the site of corporate headquarters nor of the many service delivery organisations which provide for the community. It is a company town with just over a quarter of a million people, mostly employed by the public services, the defence forces, the universities, or in servicing the population.

Politicians fly in for a sitting period of two or three weeks and fly home for weekends. Few live there as their seats and constituencies are elsewhere and have to be tended. Senior Cabinet members spend more time there and a few move their families there as well. But for most, and their staffers, their time in Canberra is spent in Parliament House, airports and then planes. When a decision was made to reduce night sitting hours, many backbenchers protested as they had no idea how to occupy their time if they were not involved in evening work.

Cabinet meetings and ministers' work styles leave little space for touching the real world. Their workplace is very time demanding and clubby, with relationships between groups, such as factions, replacing most other forms of friendship.

Decisions are made in many settings but these are rarely conducive to good outcomes, with the long hours and artificiality of the settings making the atmosphere very detached from the outside world.

Not surprisingly many mistakes are made, enough to fill a book in themselves. These occur not just in local politics but range widely through government and business ranks. The role of the World Bank and of major financial institutions, the wars such as the Gulf War and other such macho exercises including the Falklands, indicate that international cultures of decision making are flawed and limited, even if female leaders are sometimes involved.

The prevalence of a macho decision-making structure puts the world at risk, often because the focus is on the magic bottom line. The processes of decision making, and the limits of the experiences of the main decision makers, raises for me a very real fear that much of the direction of the last few years has been potentially damaging for civilisation as we still know it. I am not claiming that had women been there we would necessarily have made a difference. Obviously Margaret Thatcher did not as she acted well within the existing framework, and in fact enhanced it by further extending it with macho actions. I am, however, suggesting that part of the problem is the general uniformity of views and backgrounds of those in power. Senior managers in governments or elsewhere are likely to come from privileged backgrounds, educated at elite universities, often in the limited disciplines of current dominant economics, and protected from dealing with people and everyday life.

There is a theory propounded in management courses that

errors are made in decisions because of the phenomenon of 'groupthink'. This is the process which occurs in groups such as Cabinets and boards when the participants tend to be fairly similar in views and experience, and where the organisational culture emphasises loyalty and agreement. By staying within their comfort zone, the 'leaders' don't have to risk being challenged, and even serious errors are endorsed because no one wants to be the spoiler.

Taking advice only from those likely to agree with you, puts you at serious risk of getting something wrong. The well-respected Emeritus Professor Charles Lindblom from Yale wrote of this in his essays 'Still Muddling', in 1959 and 1969.[11] He claims that good decisions come from seeking advice from those likely to be opposed to what you want to do; that 'mutual partisan adjustment' is the key as it ensures that opposing and differing views are heard.

A case can easily be made to suggest that errors in economic and social judgment are the result of a groupthink process in which there was a belief that 'there is no alternative'. The convergence, until very recently, of Government and Opposition policies at the federal level in Australia suggests that there were few opposing views considered to be legitimate.

The exclusion of any particular class or group from decision making increases the likelihood of mistakes being made. The particular culture of senior managers, if too definably masculine, can actively undermine any broader input into decisions and change. If women have to operate within current masculine terms our value is reduced.

In a slim volume, *Trials at the Top*,[12] Amanda Sinclair explores how Chief Executives talk about men, women and the Australian executive culture. Her interviews with eleven very senior CEOs, who are all men, confirm in their words some of the assertions I have made here. 'The Australian Executive culture is most commonly described by Chief Executives as "a man's world"—not just the domain of men, but "in a general sense of the culture . . . a male oriented type of interaction".'

Sinclair identifies two masculine cultures operating—presumably a factor of age and class—patrician elite clubbiness and locker room larrikinism. One interviewee says: 'It's all male . . . everyone gets invited to the same things . . . it's the same people all the time talking to each other and that does not promote change very well. It does not drive change and that's the real issue.'

The terms used by the men interviewed are also significant. They talk about the rat race, taking body blows, giving stick, clawing at the door, and other combat related terms. This raises serious issues of whether warrior mentality and culture are what is required in senior management. The command models, the concepts of group loyalty, and the often used processes of hazing to create unquestioning discipline still operate in boardrooms in varying forms. These are not concepts that fit with a future management system based on new ideas and inclusivity.

## Refitting the images

An article in *The Australian*[13] illustrates the problems for women and their visibility. The topic was the decision of Anna Booth not to move to Melbourne to pursue a senior union career. The treatment the story had received earlier in the week was already an indication of how prominent women are too often defined as representative, rather than individual; that what one woman does is generalised to include all women.

Anna Booth's decision made headlines and received considerable coverage on all media. An ABC interviewer asked her in a tone more suited to a sports program, 'Weren't you hungry enough?' This implication, that senior managers who are not sharks will not and should not survive, is quite a frightening indication of what is expected at that level. Her response showed her acceptance of some of the unrealistic expectations. She said that she would continue working ten hours a day, but just would not be moving cities.

*The Australian* article continued these themes in slightly more polite terms. The opening paragraph explains both her senior position and her 'glamour girl' of the Australian union movement status. It goes on:

*Since revealing her decision on Monday, Booth (40) has been astonished at the media interest—newspapers, morning radio, national television. Her move has been widely interpreted as a sign that the union movement is unfriendly to women or that, after all, Booth's superwoman image was illusory. Motherhood and high-powered careers are indeed incompatible. 'The fact that you can be accused of selling out, or backing off or letting the side down for making a personal career choice is evidence that equality does not exist,' Booth argues. She knows several men in the union movement who would or have made the same decisions for the same reasons, not wishing to uproot their families. 'But no one was running around interviewing them and saying they were wimping out,' she observes.*

The article noted that there were only six women on the ACTU executive then. Now one of them, Jennie George, is the first woman president of the ACTU. The relative scarcity of women in these senior ranks makes any action they take seem significant.

This has been illustrated by the difficulties of two Cabinet ministers in the Keating government. Without canvassing the reasons for the problems faced by Ros Kelly and Carmen Lawrence, there is no doubt that in both cases, their being, at that time, the only woman in Cabinet made their problems more newsworthy and the Opposition pressure more joyous.

If the Cabinet included four or five women, one in trouble would have been treated in the same way as a man in the same situation. The only woman creates a symbol that other women and journalists see as representing all women, or at least all women interested in politics. As long as the 'one woman' situation continues—the odd woman, the exceptional one—women in these situations will be 'at risk'. Their problems will be seen as indicating that women can't make it, or that there is something wrong with a woman who does make it.

For example, the release of the film *Little Women* brought a spate of coverage of the director, Gillian Armstrong. In *The Australian Magazine*,[14] journalist Michelle Gunn, ruminating on her subject's career, wrote:

*Unusually imposing for someone with such fine facial features, the matriarch [at 44!] of Australian film is often described as tough and aggressive. It's a myth, she says, that has persisted since the filming of her debut feature,* My Brilliant Career, *in 1978. In those days the first woman to make a film in Australia for 50 years, she was a curiosity, and like many women who have achieved success in male-dominated fields, she was assigned the character traits of men ... 'I was a woman director, it was rare those days, so it was assumed I must be strong and aggressive ... There was a certain pressure doing* My Brilliant Career *... it wasn't just could Gill Armstrong do it, it was could women do it? So that was a huge burden to carry'.*

While women are still rarities in senior ranks, the pressure on them to represent all other women remains. Their personal lives are under scrutiny, their behaviour as managers, as women and as whatever else, is subjected to constant comparisons. This indicates that we have a long way to go before there are enough of us to become invisible and part of the general organisational culture.

Yet these stories sometimes point to the different experiences women have and the benefits of these. How many men drop children off at school on their way to work, or have to deal with their needs whilst at work? When I am talking about family roles, I use an example to illustrate the differences in experiences. This is a not uncommon, two-income family where he leaves the house at 7 am and returns at 8 pm, leaving her to do the tasks connected with home and family before she arrives at work at 9 am. In the five extra hours per day she spends on family activities, before and after her paid job, she necessarily stays in touch with the way the world operates, and he potentially loses all sense of it.

This tale of the differences between the roles of parents in such households carries a punchline. *She* is the one who deals with screaming children, the need for a funny hat for the school play, the school lunches, the fights, the drama of missing sports uniforms, the tensions and problems of delivering two small people to school and child care, all the while planning the dinner and getting to work on time.

The reversed process at night, including what Geraldine Doogue calls the arsenic hour, requires considerable resources to deal with tired self and children, the household needs, often work brought home, and the needs of non-resident family and friends. Yet these are seen as of less value than the comparative comfort of the senior executive tasks the male performs at that time. Why is *he* the one seen as having had the long, hard day?

The value placed on what *he* does in running the workplace is higher than that placed on domestic chores. Having experienced both, I am often to be heard muttering that making policy and running the country is much easier than managing a household. This is because the work is defined and prepared in ways which make it possible to finish tasks sequentially and concentrate on what is at hand. The nature of household work is that it is synchronic, all over the place and constant.

The question we should ask is, what can be gained by having input into decision-making processes from a variety of spheres? I would not suggest that major decisions be instantly devolved to a suburban playgroup or *kaffee klatsch* but we must look at better ways of evaluating skills and workloads.

CHAPTER 5

# How Women Can
## Make a Difference

Women need to rework the way leadership operates. To do this
we must evaluate the risks and benefits such a process entails.
In bringing about this change we have to take risks, to be less
sensitive about rejection, and able to deal with issues as well as
feelings. We do not have to accept inappropriate and competitive
models of leadership, but develop alternatives. At the same time
we should not reject all the existing models out of hand.

The way many institutions are presently run is unacceptable.
Our businesses, communities and governments need new directions. Therefore, I believe that women must take their turn at
leadership. Without our input, decisions will continue to be
made which ignore our concerns and which may also fail to
create the future we want. We need to start making a difference
by being in a position to set the agenda.

I would like to see a serious debate on what women could
do with power and resources. There are women in the trade and
aid areas and some who have made forays into politics. There
have been moves to put more women into parliaments and into
corporate boardrooms, but these argue for the inclusion of
women as a matter of equity, not because we might have something different to say.

In the 1960s and 1970s, it was logical to ask those in power, mainly men, to fix things for us. We lobbied, demonstrated and applied pressure and had many successes. Nevertheless, the changes we achieved have not affected the relative power of men and women, nor the overall status of women.

As indicated in the Introduction, there are many more women in the paid workforce now, more women in parliaments, and more women in senior ranks of the public service. This is not just an Australian pattern but is happening fairly widely in the western world. Our numbers in these positions have increased but the distribution of power and resources still has not shifted significantly. Now we have to be prepared to take on our share of this power, even if those who currently hold it are resistant to sharing it.

## Changing the rules—and rulers

We have to develop an acceptance of strong women as leaders and sources of new ideas. At present there are particularly savage controls on powerful women who play in masculine ways. They are punished, when men are not, for their inappropriate leadership behaviour. Women who behave in hierarchical, non-consultative ways, who demand services, forget their manners occasionally, blame others and lack good communication skills are seen as sinning far more grievously than men who do exactly the same things. Even when they act in ways which mirror their male peers or are less offensive, women are often judged more severely.

This sets up a very narrow stereotype and condemns women to failure. When this is combined with an assumption that many women in leadership positions will also immediately and publicly raise feminist issues, it becomes even more absurd. Very few radical feminists would survive the selection process and few other women would be prepared to sacrifice their careers by being seen to be pushing political barrows.

The modes of dealing with those who are working for you are valued in management. But there is more to leadership than management skills alone. We must look at other issues such as the ability to work with peers, the capacity to sort and retrieve appropriate information, and to synthesise this material. Managers need to be skilled in lateral thinking and creative ideas, moving the group into new areas and ways of thinking without scaring the horses. Leadership is about risk taking, challenging the status quo and often persisting with new ideas until they become acceptable.

Most of these skills involve elements of behaviour that are not generally accepted as feminine. However, they are also possibly some of the traits needed to ensure ideas are heard. Given these contradictions it is not surprising that in the period of just over a hundred years since women were given the vote with women's suffrage in South Australia, so few women have become political leaders, candidates or members of Parliament. Now, political parties are making commitments to increase the proportion of women members before the year 2002. The pressure for more senior women on boards continues in business and the public service, with many pious hopes that women will move up; there are definite signs of progress but starting from a low base.

For the last three decades we have tried to explain to those in power what they were doing wrong; we have offered our critiques and our assistance. In 1975, the United Nation's International Women's Year officially recognised the problems faced by women, and governments have since taken on some of the concerns raised. There is in place now, in Australia at least, a range of advisory committees, Equal Employment Opportunities (EEO) units and other apparatus for providing input on women's needs.

It is important that we articulate why we are pushing for the inclusion of women in the structures of the State, the economy and other powerful institutions. Is it just an equality issue (defined by an ex boss of mine as 'we will have equality when there as many idiotic senior women as there are males')? Do we focus on altering the gender mix, assuming that this factor alone will change the organisation? Do we, explicitly or implicitly, believe that more women means that changes will be made in the way institutions will work?

We 1970s feminists can claim with pride the initial creation of the various structures and strategies for EEO and Women's Studies that now exist. There is an entire human rights industry which women have had a big part in creating, and many of the mechanisms designed by women have been used by other outgroups to put their claims. But although these are great achievements, they are not why I and many others committed ourselves to being public feminists and difficult women. We didn't want merely an entree into male worlds, nor just to share the spoils of power, or to simplistically broaden women's choices to include what men do.

We have to take on a more specific role, articulating our objectives and the means by which we can achieve them. This will shift our concerns from looking at what has happened to women, per se, to what can be explained by the absence of women and feminist perspectives.

## Are women essentially different?

I want to tackle the crucial issue of 'difference'. In the practical sphere of the debate on women in leadership there are two major implications: whether women are wired differently so they can be relied on to provide different types of input; and whether this difference precludes women working within current masculine structures.

If we assume that difference is natural and permanent, there is a temptation to allocate responsibilities on this basis; if it is a product of society then it presumably will change over time and we have some control over what the changes might be. This is one of the big debates at any conference of women; will women, as women, make a difference, or is it feminism or other 'isms', that will affect outcomes.

There is a large body of academic work which has explored theories of difference. These came from some interesting theorising about the way that gender, culture, class and race, for instance, inhibit the capacity of dominant groups to speak on behalf of minorities. The critiques of broad generalisations made on behalf of categories of people have worked to correct often simplistic assumptions. In some cases, these critiques have encouraged previously silent groups to find their own voices and make their own cases.

The effects of debates on difference have had mixed results for women. There has been a greater awareness of the difference between women and more respect for listening to voices from the less powerful and articulate. There are also downsides as the fragmentation of categories has made it often harder to speak with a unified voice even strategically.

There is, however, a need to remember that the category *woman* has no more use than that of *man*. Both cover the spectrum of human experiences, with many overlapping and different characteristics. There are very obvious male and female attributes such as chromosome patterns (XX and XY) but even here there are anomalies. The great difference between men and women is our capacity to bear children and the physical apparatus this requires. But it is very important to remember that there are women who do not have this capacity, and others who choose not to have children. This does not make them 'not women'.

Some feminists claim that there are essential sex differences. That is, there are sufficient significant inborn characteristics which make the category *woman* essentially different to the category *man*. The extreme political outcome of this stance is separatism, which is that we need separate spheres and processes for men and women, boys and girls. What suits one may not suit the other, and the levels of difference agreed to exist may require very different treatments. The defining characteristic of essentialist theories is that they assume that what is inborn is generally immutable, or at least hard to change. Therefore essentialists would maintain that women are likely to make different decisions if given power. However, they may also raise issues of whether women will want or accept the male version of power.

There has always been the view that women are closer to nature than men, and as we are potential child bearers, this gives us a lien on a more organic set of relationships, not only to family but to 'mother' nature. This differentiation appears early in the classical writings and allowed male philosophers to relegate women to the savage, primitive, less developed, pre-modern realm.

Men, on the other hand, have been defined as civilised or able to be civilised by the process of State control, science and knowledge. The modern State built on a model of progress is the creation of man, and assumes the exclusion of women.[1] The differentiation of roles is common: the expressive being female and the instrumental being male, as theorised by Talcott Parsons; or Durkheim's claim that the difference came from the smaller size of women's brains.

These would just be interesting byways into histories of ideas if they were not still powerful and controlling images today. There are many debates amongst feminists about the differences between women. While some of these relate to cultural diversity, others draw from the nature/nurture debate and place women back in the primitive again.

Some of the rhetoric of EEO has inadvertently and deliberately pushed the idea that women are intrinsically different and that our leadership will be of the cuddly and caring variety. This has also received support from the 'biology as destiny' separatist feminists. So we are left with another form of stereotyping which juxtaposes essential macho management against essential feminine cosiness.

I do not believe that women leaders will create a utopia of peace and love. Even if we are the birth givers and carers, I do not believe that we are programmed genetically to be 'good'. Women leaders are not going to guarantee a warm and mothering government as we are as capable as men are of being authoritarian, corrupt and even cruel. We have just had fewer opportunities to misuse power.

We have only to look at the records of some of the women who have made it into leadership positions. I once heard someone say that Maggie Thatcher was to feminism what Idi Amin was to the black movement. It was both a joke and a useful corrective to those who assume that either race or gender has any 'natural' claims on social or ethical virtues or vices.

I believe that we arrive with certain genetic and social potential and it is the lives we live, our social environment mixed with our genetic make-up that will determine who we are. The relative contributions of nature and nurture will probably never be precisely determined but we have ample evidence of man's capacity for good and evil, and of woman's ability to span a similar range.

As long as women's experiences, our responsibilities and our ways of being in the world are different, so will our viewpoints and ideas be different. There is no clear definition of what is female versus male, as it differs through time and across cultures. There is, however, an acceptance of gender differences within cultures of men's and women's socially constructed roles.

Where women are involved in decision making they bring these different social experiences to the tasks. For the next decade at least, the current gender differences will ensure that women retain a major part of the child rearing and care nexus. So as long as we are still allocated different roles and power relationships, most of us will bring alternative views into any senior level forums.

There are many examples of this, but a few from *The Australian* newspaper early in 1995, indicate both what women have achieved and what we still have to do. The ACT election for the small, Parliament/Council which rules the national capital Canberra, had two female party leaders standing for the position of Chief Minister. 'Both argued that being women had not changed the way politics is run in the ACT Assembly but their presence has influenced the agenda,' the article read.

The article mentions the issues dealt with: child care, parental leave, support for carers and sexual harassment control were all on the agenda. Another member commented that one of the two candidates did the soft bits, leaving her male colleagues to do the head kicking, but acknowledged the other woman did her own. So there are differences between women.

Another article in the same newspaper by Susan Wyndham on the making of the film *Little Women*, picks up similar themes.

It starts with the sub-heading 'Gillian Armstrong places her motherly stamp on Little Women'. Later in the article, there is a description of the set:

*The* Little Women *set was aswarm with children—Armstrongs, Sarandons, Dinovis and Swicords—and with the large cast of women together for three months, there was an unusual degree of female bonding.*

*'I try to build up the actors' trust so they feel safe and can do anything, and you are there and you love them and will choose their best moments,' says Armstrong. 'I also choose my crew very carefully because you can't create this wonderful atmosphere in rehearsal, then suddenly have all these loud technicians clumping around and laughing just after somebody's done a very sensitive take.'*

*An 11-year-old member paid Armstrong the compliment of comparing her to a mother: 'She's so intelligent, so loving and relaxed, she made the set very calm and relaxed.'*

This contrasts with an earlier quote by Wyndham in the same article, which paints Gillian Armstrong's more 'masculine' traits, exemplifying the differences in the way one woman can be portrayed in the media.

### On the one hand

These examples indicate that the presence of women often does and can make a difference to both content and process. However, this cannot be read as 'natural' and needs to be considered mutable and therefore socially determined. I am always concerned when it is assumed by both women and men that women in senior positions will contribute the interpersonal relationship skills that are needed in the workplace. It is important to recognise that gender-based assumptions serve neither group.

There are obviously men who have problems with the current macho styles of behaviour and consequently find that they are not seen as promotion material. The man who takes parental leave or follows his wife's career moves will be seen as womanish, that is, not really serious about his career. It is interesting to note that behaving in what are defined as feminine ways does endanger men, but that women who behave in masculine ways are given very mixed messages as some succeed and others fail as a result of similar behaviour.

Women in some jobs may be admired for 'being as good as a man', and others find their efforts are seen as threatening and they are punished for what is regarded as inappropriately aggressive behaviour. However, it is important to state clearly here that selling ourselves as 'good women', as agents of influence who will do the men's emotional housework in the workplace, is also a very bad idea. It has two serious disadvantages. The first is that the stereotypical women will be allocated a very narrow band of authority and functions. In Helen Lynch's paper[2] she list a series of questions about where the women are in senior ranks. The answer is that most are in human resources or marketing, in other words, what are seen as soft areas; few run the power sections of treasury and finance.

The second problem with being defined as feminine managers is that many women cannot deliver what is expected as we have neither a bent for feminised occupations, nor are we good emotional managers. Of course, there will be very successful marketeers and human resource managers who will do well. However, they may find their paths to other jobs restricted and their behaviour monitored to make sure they deliver the stereotypical skills.

Women are often judged harshly if they fail on the human skills and are treated like an idiot savant if they trespass into male domains. Frequently, undermined senior women find they are accused of lacking people management skills and so are seen to fail not only in their jobs but as a woman.

It is hardly surprising that many senior women will and are leaving the mainstream to run their own firms. As part of the sideline they have little power to make serious changes to the direction of powerful institutions. We lose numbers when women leave and this means also that fewer women are likely to move up into senior ranks. The turnover rates of women in senior management are higher than those of men as women find the culture uncomfortable or limiting. And, as always in caring jobs, women sometimes fail to meet expectations as they are really better suited, as are some men, to more task-oriented jobs.

Masculine models offer a view of the world where everything is ordered and sequential, and decisions are made on the basis of a particular form of rationality, logic and documentation. Such ordered views produce the fiction that outcomes are easy to predict and that given the right information the correct decisions will be made.

The alternative has its own problems. An understanding of the complexities of life may be better gained from dealing with the chaos of everyday living, where decisions are taken on the run, and constantly amended as new information comes to light. However, if we become mired in the minutiae, this can reduce the possibilities of considering the bigger picture, and being able to generalise from the particular.

There are good reasons to assume that the world is both ordered by our views and chaotic, so a mixture of both may provide the best training for good management and good leadership. Assuming decisions are simple at either level is not appropriate.

Too much of the unstructured life, and the person may well find dealing with the comparative order of the workplace too hard. Some women find the level of discipline required to work cooperatively with other adults or under someone's supervision very difficult after the relative self-direction of the household.

Also, too much of the world outside the boardroom may be seen by some as threatening and incomprehensible. The order of the workplace may offer an alternative to home and community and be sufficiently powerful to make long hours a pleasure and time in the office, away from home, may be a recreation rather than a necessity. Certainly the culture of some organisations suggests that those who prefer home and family to the community of the workplace, whether male or female, may be seen as somewhat odd and not serious members of that work force.

# PART TWO

1976

Nothing Miss Bell – I just needed to feel powerful....

1996

Nothing Ms Bell – I just needed to feel powerful...

## CHAPTER 6

# Mirror,
# Mirror on the Wall

Who is the fairest of us all? I do not mean the common association of beauty desired by Snow White's wicked stepmother but fair in the sense of fair play, in relation to other women. The proposition I will explore here is that we are, too often, unfair in our judgment of each other, and therefore are active participants in the process of gender injustice. When reading the following chapters you need to understand the assumption that we live in a specifically masculine designed society, which has severely inhibited both the progress of women and the potential for improvements in the directions the world is taking. I believe that an increased number and a more diverse range of women can make a positive difference to these directions as they gain positions of leadership and power. But to be really effective we first need to identify the problems we make for ourselves and other women and then, look at why many of us fail in our use of power.

I know that I have been guilty of unfairness to other women and have been treated unfairly myself by other women. My own experiences compelled me to think it through and note what I have seen happen to others, so I feel I am in a position to write on this subject. This is risky because the media and critics love a cat fight and will be looking for opportunities to set up any criticisms they can find in this book for a re-run of the Helen Garner and *The First Stone*[1] episode.

There is an interesting point to be drawn from the media attention given to the Garner book, which is a partial account of complaints of sexual harassment laid against the Master of Ormond College, at Melbourne University. Garner's judgment was not seen as a legitimate, if minor debate within feminism. It was defined as a significant and potentially damaging battle between the ideologies of generations. This prominent and excessive interest in such critiques makes me uncertain of the reception for my criticisms of the actions of some women.

Yet we must be able to talk about the problems we cause ourselves and each other. This does not mean that the problems I identified in Part One are our fault. It does mean however, that in solving these, we must take the responsibility for some of the outcomes and be careful about how we do this.

This section of the book relates primarily to the way we treat each other—within personal space, workplaces and organisations. The focus here will be on interpersonal behaviour, which can be seen to be the power process writ small, reflecting in everyday power plays the institutional framework in which we all live.

I acknowledge my belief that it is the power of the institutions in our society that determines how we make sense of ourselves individually and our world. In challenging this power we can change both our own behaviour and the impact of the institutions. Some feminists argue, as did Anees Jung,[2] an Indian writer, that it is enough to change your personal environment and actions, to model these changes and the rest—the changes to the power base of society—will come to pass as the numbers grow. I am impatient, but also scared that too many people will be harmed waiting for these changes; I want to see major reforms and sooner rather than later.

I do recognise, however, that these will not be sustained unless we first recognise the need for developing support structures for other women. There is a prevailing set of beliefs that women as nurturers are conditioned to deliver a more cooperative, life-affirming and gentle mode of living. I wish it were so. Instead I am suggesting that by responding to the masculinity drummers, the allocated spheres of approved womanhood and limited accepted behaviours, women are often co-opted into being more assiduous gatekeepers for current masculine values than are the male guardians.

Because we are often trained in the skills of interpersonal bonding we can use these skills powerfully to create controls on other women. We do not set up society's standards but often enforce them and, because we have less control over change, we are often averse to it and want to avoid conflict. We can play the role of God's police[3] as well as making use of the power of victim.

This is not a blaming exercise. I recognise why this is so often the process, and see its origins in our basic condition of Other. This is a term used to set up a duality between the category that determines the 'universal' and those defined as different. Ien Ang[4] discusses the way that white/western is a category which defines all not-white, western people as Other. Similarly, 'male' as norm defines 'woman' as a category which is unitary. Therefore, the fact that one woman's failure (or two or three) is attributed to all women identifies the Otherness of the category woman, while one man is never proof of the failure of all men.

Otherness is a moving category defined by the position of the speaker/writer. Ang sees white, western women as closer to white, western men than non-western, non-white women who are often lumped together under the category NESB (of Non English Speaking Background). These views reinforce our differences.

## Victims can be powerful

One of the problems we face in trying to change the world, is that women have been discouraged from developing some of the skills needed to do so. This is the paradox of powerlessness: it may give us a perspective on the world that is missing from the decisions being taken, but it also deprives us of the training we need to be effective.

This creates a further paradox which I call the comfort of the victim. There is an often quite unrecognised power in the role of victim: victims cannot be further hurt and by making their status clear, the potential perpetrator of possible harm may be immediately removed from control over the situation. So the woman who announces that no one ever listens to her suggestions before making a decision creates both guilt and annoyance, but may still be ineffective.

Some women develop the victim power process as a response

to their powerlessness. It allows them to express their fear of becoming a victim in a way which is acceptable. By mimicking the genuine powerlessness that does affect many women, we can sometimes deflect anger or express our own anger in acceptable ways. This is one of the major hurdles women face in looking at the ways we interact.

The first section of this book acknowledged the harm done by both structural discrimination and by men who may be misogynists, unaware or simply insensitive. Changing men will be hard, so women first need to change what we do to ourselves and to each other, as well as to men.

This part of the book is treading on dangerous ground. In being critically aware of what we can and do do to each other, I am worried this material will be seen as vinegar not honey and be too sour to pursue. But I hope instead that it generates debate and productive conflict and allows us to prove that we can take on criticisms, and make relevant changes. This does not mean women are to blame, but that we have taken on the responsibilities for fixing what we can.

### Women on women

Think about the last few weeks: about women you work with, or other women work with; about women in the public eye; about women in senior jobs; about a woman above you at work or someone who is going for promotion; about women in your social scene, or women you know through community contacts. Listen to the words you or others have used in talking about them, any of them. Have you discussed them, judged them differently from the way you would a man; has anyone you talked to done this?

It is all right to make different judgments, everyone is different. But are you sure that you were even-handed or could it be you were tougher on the woman than you would be on a man? Think about male bosses, male public figures, males in senior positions. How do you discuss men? Do you discuss men? Do you gripe about them as often, or as angrily, as you do about women in similar positions?

Think back over the past few months and see if you can identify times when you have found the behaviour of one or more women particularly irritating, or inept, unfeeling or too bossy. Would you have been as annoyed by comparable behaviour in men?

Would you give brownie points to a man who had to leave work early on a busy day to do the children's pick-up run, but feel less impressed by a woman in the same situation? Would you react differently to bad temper, or lack of sympathy from a senior woman than you would from a man? Do you expect more personal interaction and support from a woman than a man in similar situations? Do you expect her to be more patient and forbearing?

Have you ever resented other women's capacity to speak out and engage in arguments? Do you sometimes feel pushy women are worse than pushy men? Do you pass judgment on how women look, what they wear and how they behave, but fail to notice similar aspects of men?

I can plead guilty to all the above, except maybe resenting other women who take risks I am not prepared to take. I have bitched about other women, been part of sessions bagging women in power, and have been angry at the odd feminist who has not done her duty as I defined it. So join me in the sin bin and let us explore how this criticism works against us. If you expect women to be better than men, you may be discriminating against them. If you have ever been angry at women for behaviour acceptable in men, then it's possible that you are part of the problem women face. I doubt whether any of us could claim never to have been guilty of discriminatory behaviour or thinking.

I now feel wary of joining any of the trampling tall poppy sessions. Partly this comes from my own experiences moving up and down the system, and in and out of it. I know it is not easy up or out there. It also comes from my perception of what is happening to many other women. When I count the number of women who survive in senior ranks, there are few. When I raise the issue of the support they receive from other women there are expressions of wry amusement and some pain. There are also accounts of immensely loyal friendships and workmates, which show we carry the contradictions within us.

I see how we can both inadvertently and deliberately become co-opted into the process of controlling other women. By being more critical and prescriptive about women, both conservative and radical, women undermine others who try to break away from the confines set by sexist precepts.

I want to look at how we can reduce the level of women on women criticism. When I put this proposition, I often receive bemused and sometimes hostile responses. There is an assumption that women are nicer than men, and certainly there are widespread beliefs amongst feminists and others, that we are generally supportive of other women.

Usually the initial reaction is followed by recognition that women are often critical of other women. In a different response some women ask, 'Are you saying we can't criticise any other women?' or shrug off the comment with, 'Not that 1970s sisterhood stuff! Supporting other women as though they can do no wrong ignores the real differences between us'.

I am not suggesting we become unnaturally sweet and nice to one another in a caricature of femininity. I am not suggesting that women always have to agree with other women, regardless of what they say. Nor am I advising that as feminists, we cannot criticise other feminists. Far from this, I believe that we must be able to label and condemn behaviour by both women and men that is inappropriate and sexist. If we didn't we would be part of the process which stifles change, as many desirable reforms come from debates and critiques.

I am advocating a fair go, to ensure that we do not judge women more harshly than we would men for similar behaviour. We have all recognised the double standards that men apply to women, particularly in sexual behaviour. What we have not named and identified as clearly is the way women judge other women.

This is not a version of the older mythologies I grew up with, which assumed that women were naturally 'bitchy' or 'catty' and too competitive for male attention to be genuinely friendly with each other. I am identifying a much more complex set of phenomena which involve women needing to review their group and individual relationships with other women. These often incorporate mixed assumptions about appropriate womanly behaviours that establish or reinforce stereotypes not applied to men.

Another important issue for women is the way we often deal with criticisms. There is evidence[5] that women are more likely to take criticism personally, and thus are more adversely affected by it. If we are scared of being criticised we are less likely to attempt change.

There are times when we all deserve some criticism and we must be able to deal with it without feeling unloved or too personally under attack. I would suggest that this problem is sometimes more acute in groups committed to advocacy. I have little experience of conservative or right radical groupings of women, but I suspect they demand a relatively unquestioned allegiance to both policies and acceptable behaviour.

Having been part of many feminist groups, and having spent much of my time in the last two decades in the company of formal and informal groups of women, I am aware of both the problems and possibilities. I have had a multitude of exciting, cooperative, collegiate times working with and for women. I also know of, and have experienced, too many situations where women, present and absent, are subjected to unfair and damaging attacks from other women.

Of course men do this too. I have worked in mixed groups within male-dominated organisations where men have been undermined and destroyed for their failure to conform. My point is that the politics and violence of male group processes can be challenged. It is much harder to do this and seek changes in the way women act towards each other because it is not part of the discourses on women. We need to decide whether we are applying some feminine, or even some feminist, criteria too heavily and thereby likely to discourage other women from taking chances and making changes.

In the same way that we define harassment as verbal and emotional, not just physical, we need to recognise that women are capable of perpetrating emotional violence on each other. The power of this is increased when our actions reflect values and ideas that we have absorbed as the subordinate group in an unevenly gendered society. These are not ideas that have developed amongst women, or within women's groups. They are largely the result of dominant gender assumptions about appropriate feminine behaviour, embellished and adapted through women's eyes and our responses to male demands. We have to move from defining ourselves via men to developing ways of validating ourselves through our own perceptions. We can then see the value of our diversities as well as our similarities.

I do not expect women to be saints. This would be another universalising assumption about an outgroup. It is important to recognise that the pace of change has been rapid, but not fast enough for us to move away from certain negative aspects of feminine culture and habits. These stay intact or transmute into some difficult and negative forms of female behaviour.

## The unkindest cut

The unkindest cut of all comes from someone we expected to be our supporter; the worst betrayals are from those we trust. The judgments we impose on ourselves limit our possibilities. If we criticise other women for failing male standards, or for failing to meet unrealistic alternate feminist or feminine standards we give real comfort to those who oppose us.

When I was growing up the expectation was that we would not have many women friends and the ones we did have were to gossip with. Women then sought the company of men for serious discussions, assuming other women wanted to talk just about babies and recipes. This has changed now and groups of women are acceptable sources of company and serious conversation. But men still exert a powerful influence on what women value and what we would like to see in other women.

Whenever women act as guardians of the status quo, we do a very effective job because we are trained to have power over people's feelings, particularly those of other women. So when some women choose or inadvertently make it hard for those who opt for different choices and challenges to male hegemony, they act as agents for male dominance.

In all areas of a dominant and underling culture, there are rewards for those supporting the powerful. The peculiarly interdependent nature of men and women means that compliance— acceptance of the status quo—has some considerable benefits, providing a pragmatic means of achieving a level of reflected, if not direct, power.

Women can discriminate against women, or men, by ascribing to either group certain positive or negative qualities which categorise and limit their options because of their gender. We are all familiar with the standard assumptions about natural femininity and household skills, and older women will remember assumptions about digital dexterity and attention to detail which explained why so many women were typists.

However, we need to recognise that new stereotypes developed in good faith by some feminist groups can be almost as hard to conform to. Claims that women are naturally more warm and caring managers than men create different barriers to deny them entry to senior positions. Managerial women who are seen as not sufficiently caring are again in trouble for a flaw in what is nebulously called their style. The problems become worse if it is women who lead the criticism of other women.

Time and again, women tell stories of how other women have been put down or have put them down. As I move around women's groups, which I do often and widely, I find my ears ringing and my jaw tensed by hearing these groups' criticisms of others and the hurt of some. These informants come in all shapes and sizes and from all political views and positions, and the experiences they recount cannot be explained away as just the normal interchanges amongst those wanting reform.

Women on women discrimination tends to be glossed over and it is not seen as appropriate to mention it in public. When I explain I am writing about this issue the overwhelming reaction is relief that someone else is raising this problem. Suggesting that women are part of the problem, as well as the solution, is often seen as being anti-women and anti-feminist, or as following the patriarchal line. Because of this we tend to believe that we may be incorrect in our analysis or may fail to understand the occasional and expected mistakes any groups make. We need to recognise that we are active and complicit in the processes that men may initiate but that ultimately we are responsible for the way we treat each other.

Masculinity, in particular forms and applications, contains many problematic assumptions; so too does femininity. Some aspects of accepted feminine behaviour need to be changed to make women more effective leaders, without buying into the current dysfunctional models.

We do not have to wait for male permission or support as this is the area in which we have the control, power and capacity to make changes. We must look at what we can do, which is harder than claiming that changes are the responsibility of others. Women have found unity from our collective complaints about sexism. This has allowed us to avoid shouldering the responsibility for making changes to ourselves.

### 'But conflict is not feminine!'

I suspect that even if we were no longer actively discriminated against by masculine institutions, women would hold the present system in place without realising how we have internalised certain values and attitudes.

Some women find the problem of undermining the discriminatory and oppressive aspects of masculine-defined notions of power particularly difficult. The opponents in this case are not easy to spot but are those people we may share love and space with: mothers, wives, daughters and friends, many of whom identify themselves through their relationships to men.

The problems this causes often relate to the way women see

conflict. For many, conflict is in itself unacceptable, because it is either unfeminine or too masculine. For others it is too frightening so they choose to avoid it.

Many will regard women who demand change as troublemakers. By naming men as the enemy, some women are seen as creating conflicting demands for loyalty. Change often involves conflict and women may feel they have too much to lose, both by the conflict and by the changes sought. Some are burned by experience and want to be taken care of, to be protected by men because change is frightening.

Even amongst those wanting reform there are often bitter debates on how it can be achieved. Some claim, in the name of feminism, that they do not want any part of men's world and others under a similar name will seek to change it.

Whatever changes we might want to pursue, it is unlikely that the process of change or the resolution of often diverse demands can be achieved without dealing with conflict. Those who are privileged will oppose those seeking to share these privileges as a matter of course. If the avoidance of conflict is perceived as a feminine virtue, then this view must be altered if we want to be effective agents of social change.

One of the most confusing aspects for any reformist group is discovering its own internal dissensions. Finding out what is desired by the group and agreeing on how to achieve these goals makes for cohesive, clear demands. This gives right-wing, left-wing or more authoritarian or dogma based groups considerable advantages. They present a clear picture and cohesive memberships.

Those observing the movements for change tend to be highly critical of differences within and between movements, groups and individuals: differences between black groups in South Africa, disputes between older and younger feminists, and so on. There seems to be a sporting or war metaphor in place which assumes that participants are part of a team or army and must always agree or at least provide a united public face.

Most movements are not uniform or monolithic, and are often not even structured in ways that allow for the development of common policies and practices. Those groups which are defined by others and themselves as part of the women's movement cover a very broad spectrum of political views, only uniting on some key issues, and often even these are not universal.

This is not a problem, nor should it be. We do not expect uniformity in the ideas of men, so why should we expect it of women? There is even less sense in expecting the range of groups of women involved in reforms to agree on all aspects of change as by its nature, change is contentious. Feminists passionately defend their rights to difference in some spheres and push for consensus in others.

As discussed above, there are particular penalties for conflict amongst women. These are often more serious than penalties for women in conflict with men. The media delight in seeking out the possible conflicts between sections of feminisms, between feminists and the men's movement, between conservative women's groups and those deemed more radical, and between women in paid work and those who are not.

The media, and more importantly women, often fail to recognise that this very breadth of views is a strength not a weakness. We would be as ossified as the male hierarchies we oppose if we claimed we knew and agreed on all the answers. We need to be able to debate and disagree as we work towards better ways of achieving reforms.

Decisions based on dispute, debate and dissent are healthy ways of achieving the best outcomes, as they allow a range of options to be explored. Both women and men bring to any change process a variety of cultures and backgrounds. However, because of our experiences as women we share certain similarities. The female responsibilities set us up for care and nurture, and the traditional and social limitations that arise from these can cross class, race and culture.

I do not accept the assumption that women are naturally more caring and less likely to aggress and compete. This is an aspect of socialisation and varies within and across cultures. In the Anglo-European models, women have fewer opportunities for public aggression and are not rewarded for competitive behaviour. We are therefore more likely to make use of the modes for resolution of conflicts.

We need to look at our own capacities to deal with aberrant behaviours, those not seen as feminine or feminist. We may find that many of the behaviours ascribed to women have their own downside. Nurturing and care skills may involve elements of control and demands for small group conformity. These can militate against dissent, risk taking and new ideas.

We tend to complain about what we do not like, but often

find looking for solutions more difficult. For women this may be partly explained by the way those of us in anglophone countries deal with differences. I have noticed women in groups often finding the process of disagreement more worthy of attention than the content.

Solving differences by war and aggression is not functional, nor is the suppression of differences. This is why we must amalgamate elements from what are seen as male and female behaviours and make something new. I firmly believe that we need dissent and debate to determine what changes are necessary, and to find ways of implementing them that are not destructive. As we achieve change we must continue to question and review the directions we take. This requires us to deal with both internal and external pressures that influence the way we interact with other women.

Conflict within and between women's groups is framed as evidence that women are not suitable reformers. If they cannot get their own households in order, how can they be seen as legitimate in trying to change the world? This discourse assumes that women in conflict are somehow demeaned in ways which men in conflict are not.

The public and the media delight in setting up conflicts between feminists and this can create paranoia and anxiety amongst women's groups. Consequently, the groups move defensively to close ranks and appear to offer a uniform set of responses. Part of this is the usual action taken by less powerful groups when they feel under attack, but more importantly it is an attempt to conform to a stereotype that sees women as the peaceable sex.

This debate offers a view of one of the major problems women face. The myths of femininity provide a potential stranglehold on and obstruction to achieving what we want. This happens as we internalise the images of what is a 'good woman' and these are most effectively policed when women do unto each other what they fear to do to themselves.

## Angry, aggro, no no

There is a cultural fear of strong women; one of the problems we face is the lack of hero(in)es to make us comfortable with taking on some of their attributes. If women are frightened by the concept of power, and punish those women who try to assert it, we have a major problem.

Anger in women is not acceptable. It suggests that women are betraying their 'innate' nature. Shrew, hag, nag, virago, scold, termagant are all terms applied to angry women and there are no masculine equivalents. Some of these terms have now been adopted with pride by women's groups.

The Greek mythic Furies (Eumenides) were a group of very angry women who tore Orpheus apart. Their name was picked up by Charlotte Bunche and others in the 1970s as the name for a radical journal. Virago and Shrew are names of a publisher and a publication respectively but the negative connotations of these terms still exist.

Anger is often used as a derogation of feminism and as a reason why most women reject it. While rage and anger are often seen as being inappropriate for both genders, the proscription is tighter for women. On an individual basis, it means women who are angry are subject to different judgments from men in similar situations. This makes it difficult for women in senior positions as they find their outbursts are remembered while their male peers' anger is forgotten.

## Destroying difficult women

I can count at least ten senior women I know who have been sidelined despite having done excellent work in government. Most had been innovators in their areas and no criticism was ever made of their competence in their own work. Most were also pioneers—the first women in such positions or the first to hold one of the identifiably feminist positions.

While we can also list many men who did not make it, there are disturbing similarities in the fates of these women. In all cases there have been accusations that their interpersonal skills were lacking, or that they had displayed some form of anger. These accusations were used as evidence in the case for their inappropriateness as senior officers.

The women's sin of visible anger, their ability to pursue an issue with some tenacity, and their possible sins of poor people management, were seen as sufficient to publicly condemn them. Angry and committed women are almost, by definition, inappropriate senior leaders. None were regarded as ineffective; in fact some were considered to be too effective in pursuing change. There was often little else of substance that could be found against them.

So why are so many of us labelled difficult women? And how does it work? The role of other women in the process is crucial.

Most men these days will not sack or move a woman who makes them feel uncomfortable, as they are fearful that they may be seen to be discriminatory. However, with the support of other women, they can do the demolition job with a clear conscience. And chances are that the women being sidelined or downgraded are likely to accept their guilt and internalise the criticism. As a result few will even protest.

There are examples of women conforming to leadership stereotypes made by men with men in mind, who are then punished because they are women. For instance, the inattention of senior men to the needs of lower level staff may be noticed but discounted as a result of work overload. Alternatively, it will be attributed to the manner in which bosses are expected to behave. A woman deemed guilty of similar disregard is accused of poor staff management and therefore not fit to be a leader. Women are supposed to be good with people; ergo those whose people skills are limited are bad and unnatural.

It is interesting that women are rarely criticised for lack of vision, or inability to make decisions, or for poor concentration or any of the many faults I have seen in senior males. While presumably women are also guilty of some of these, this is not the basis for proving they are not good managers.

Many of the women I know, and know of, who were moved sideways or out of jobs at senior public service levels, were shifted on the excuse that they were poor managers. It is always said with a solemn air, more in sorrow than in anger, as though this was unfortunately their fatal flaw. This is a recurring theme in any discussion of women who have not 'made it'.

Women who have been unfairly chastised for being 'poor managers' or having poor people skills, often believe the criticisms. While women generally tend to accept blame and guilt more easily than men, it is particularly painful in this area because we are trained to believe that a failure in interpersonal relations, even at work, is proof we are indeed unlovable.

Few women will admit that this has happened to them, or seek to refute the often almost whispered accusations. We feel that we will be retrieved and rehabilitated and allowed some position if we show penitence and the ability to behave in an appropriately feminine manner. Conversely, any outbursts of anger and denial are seen to prove the case of unwomanly behaviour.

What goes unrecognised is that it is often women who initiate the downfall of other women. Women who work under 'unfeminine' women managers are often ready to criticise their actions although they would overlook or just grizzle about similar behaviour in men.

### Shredding the femocrats

We have developed a particular form of bureaucrat in Australia to a degree unknown in other countries. We invented the term *femocrat* to describe those women who hold jobs which have as part or all of their content, the advancement of women. There are women's units, equal opportunity units, gender equity positions and a range of complaints officer jobs. These are often outrider units in the public sector or private enterprise, although some are set up as separate statutory bodies.

Despite their relatively limited capacities to make serious changes to the main functions of their sectors, these units tend to be targeted for abolition by conservative groups, and are viewed with suspicion by many men's groups. So it is probably not surprising that any problems within them grab media headlines.

They are often areas where women managers predominate. These positions and units tend to be far less secure than other parts of the system and are often watched and disliked by power brokers opposed to equity outcomes. The managers of these units are often in difficult positions, experiencing unrealistic expectations from the community on one hand and suspicion from professional public service mandarins on the other.

Success in such a setting would require superhuman skills, and even a good performer would be at risk of failure. Sometimes incumbents have been short of a halo or two and do not do very well. Many have had the experience of being publicly bagged by the media and most have met with hostility from organised and disorganised women's groups.

This is inevitable, given the peculiar status and roles of these units. A point of concern, however, is the way the attacks come. I note that when the flak flies it is rarely, if ever, based on effectiveness or otherwise in achieving the often limited possible gains. Rather it tends to be on the basis that the woman in charge is not a good manager or she has a bad 'style'. There are stories about shouting, about unreasonable demands and about injustices done. The criticisms are almost always of the people-based competencies of the woman in charge. In some cases the criticisms are probably accurate. There are incompetent and mediocre women in senior positions, just as there are men. Not all women can be exemplary, and this expectation is in itself a problem for equity.

Again we need to remember that there are many appalling male managers in the public and private sector and, in general, they survive without being publicly pilloried. We must examine whether we should, and when we should, expect women to conform to different and more narrow prescriptions than those demanded of men. As part of a reform agenda we obviously want to validate better management and behaviour by managers. However we need to question whether it is fair or even useful to apply our criteria so tightly to women and not equivalently to men.

This does not mean that we should never question women in senior positions. Obviously there are times when it is necessary to change the person or positions. The question is how to support these women, rather than be seen to defend women inappropriately. This is difficult when there are people waiting to use any faults to undermine feminist enterprises. Therefore we need to pick our times and tactics so we do not inadvertently feed a media frenzy which may destroy the broader initiatives as well the present incumbents.

When claims of poor management are made against women I now ask myself and others involved whether we would be acting the same way were the incumbent a man. I also quiz media people who ask for my comments whether they would write the story, or even if it would be a story, if it were not a woman involved.

## CHAPTER 7

# Bad Boys
## and Bad Girls

'Bad boy' is an affectionate reprimand; it can almost be used as a term of endearment because 'boys will be boys'. 'Bad girl' carries many layers of disapproval and possible sexual overtones, and it is rarely used endearingly.

I remember many years ago, in the early 1970s, we were lobbying for changes to a law which locked up girls who were deemed to be 'potentially exposed to moral danger'. No boys were ever charged under this law; they had to be criminals to lose their liberty.

When I asked the state Minister for Child Welfare to justify this difference, he explained that 'bad boys are just going through a phase, but bad girls are really bad through and through'. This is an example of the different standards in behaviour set for females and males.

When women commit crimes we are likely to receive longer sentences than men convicted of the same offences. There is some evidence that women convicted of murder are more severely sanctioned. Men are likely to receive lighter sentences for 'crimes of passion' because they are seen as unable to control their overflow of emotion.

There is also the example of Robin Greenburg, a financial

entrepreneur from Western Australia, who established the finance group Western Women. She lost some $2–3 million and unfortunately involved a lot of women. These women had believed that Western Women was both ideologically committed to women-centred investment and run with probity.

She was sentenced to thirteen years rather than the usual couple of years or less usually given for male white-collar crime. Her sins were clear and indefensible. Without excusing what happened, the outcome for women generally was made worse because Robin was a feminist and she fell.

Her sentence after a plea of guilty stands in stark contrast to Keith Jarratt of Elders who assisted in a multimillion dollar scam and received six months and Laurie Connell who received five years for conspiracy.

There are serious questions about whether Robin Greenburg was suffering from diminished responsibility on medical grounds, given the crime was so ineptly carried out that she was bound to be caught. This raises issues about her state of mind and the justice of such a long sentence. She also confessed and therefore generally would have been treated less severely.

Interestingly, the unfairness of her sentence was not taken up by the various feminist justice groups that have lobbied against unjust sentences for other women. The difference is that most of these were sentenced for murder after domestic violence, while Greenburg ripped off other women in the name of feminism. This did not, however, justify the sentence she received.

The problem was that the case caused huge damage to more than just those who lost money. The backwash brought down other groups by association. The Women's Information Referral Service was disbanded because it had referred women to her, and anything to do with women and money has had a very bad odour since then.

Women who were duped by Greenburg, and supported her, often found difficulty in getting jobs. There were attempts to implicate the then Premier, Carmen Lawrence, because she was a woman and therefore possibly had some foreknowledge. When one woman fails using the term feminist, we are all held responsible.

## Judging women

One of the more toxic problems I have witnessed has been the reaction of many women to those of us who fall, or are pushed, from grace. There are women who did not achieve career success because we were caught between stated merit principles and actual discrimination. These are the squashed weeds I referred to in an earlier chapter, as opposed to the tall poppies who make it. If the dozens of women I know, and know of, would tell their stories, they would illustrate the hypocrisy and self-protection built into a system that claims to be merit based. This includes the compliance of many senior women in the process, who either believed or preferred to claim that the women being targeted were at fault.

I can think of few examples, since Sara Dowse, the first femocrat, resigned in protest against the downgrading of the Women's Unit in Canberra in 1976, of any senior woman making a stand on principle. Now, on my own criteria, I must state that the incidence of senior males making principled stands is equally rare, so I do not expect women to put themselves on the line.

What I am concerned about is the apparently high proportion of good and competent women who were sidelined or have left the system. Many of those who made reforms possible became victims of the process. Count the women's advisers, women in senior EEO positions, heads of women's units and others who have left the system or been moved outside their areas of expertise. Many are now working as consultants, as I was until recently; few are being effectively or appropriately used and rewarded.

This is to be expected, as there are serious risks for the few senior women employed both in femocrat and non-femocrat jobs. What is of concern, particularly when there were fairly obvious injustices, is the silence from other women who would not stand up in public support of others in case the problems were infectious.

It is not possible to tell the stories of all the women who have been rolled. Some have found different niches, others have moved into new areas where they make the best of jobs which they are not passionate about, others are still the walking wounded and their reactions range from anger to tight-lipped silence on the issue.

Most would, however, share the following experiences: of being set up with expectations that could not be met; working with extra commitment because the issues were important and they wanted results; balancing competing demands from the community and the system; and believing that despite problems, there was some commitment to making the job work from those in charge.

In both media and personal accounts I have seen a pattern of criticism that separated these women from their male peers who had similar problems. Most were horrified to find that their management style was under question. There were many reports of their failing to manage staff expertly, of shouting, of creating fear, of being too tough, and, maybe, of having poor financial management skills.

Some of these criticisms were made publicly, others privately, but the result was that outspoken women were done over. In most cases the information I received, the confidential comments and so on, were from other women in the system. Sometimes these women were themselves a party to the process.

What is rarely mentioned, and therefore underrated in these processes, is the role of other women. I have very clear memories of women reinforcing the correctness of the decisions, for example, to roll or fail to appoint many of the women in these situations. At both senior and political, and junior and community levels, women were co-opted into the decisions and validated them.

The women I know and know of, fell and moved in various ways: some failing to hold their jobs; some seeing the position upgraded and then being displaced when they applied for their own job; some finding it difficult to secure other work after resigning or finishing a contract; some being stuck in the job, labelled as difficult and finding moving up or out impossible.

Rarely, if ever, were there any substantial criticisms of the work done by these women in their organisation. This was some-what different if the unit itself was under attack. Some of the demolition jobs on equal opportunity or specialist women's units were targeted at the units as much as at the incumbent.

Of course, there are always examples of the women who have been in these situations and survived the restructuring. There are some good feminists amongst them who do push for reform and I hope they continue to succeed and move up. We need more women in senior positions as the increase in numbers will make other changes possible and more likely to happen. On the other hand, we should recognise that it is neither easy to reach a senior level nor easy to stay there, particularly if you are committed to making changes and if you pursue these visibly.

There is a limited group of very senior women who often assume that they have found the magic formulae. They need to recognise that their successes are often proof that many of the women who do succeed, do so within a much narrower range of acceptable behaviours than men.

I believe that proportionately more senior women have moved out of their jobs for the range of reasons outlined above than men. Often men are promoted as a face-saver when their incompetence emerges. It is very rare for them to be removed from jobs for lack of interpersonal skills and to be publicly labelled for it. Yet in 1994 and 1995, I can identify three women in the public eye to whom this has happened: the head of the Human Rights Commission in Queensland, the head of the New South Wales Women's Unit, and Maina Gielgud who fought to try to retain her position with the Australian Ballet.

## Mea culpa

I will not endeavour to tell the stories of individual women's successes and failures. This is neither appropriate in the case of the successful women nor possible for those who have not made it. The women concerned legitimately would not like to make their cases public, partly because some still feel they must have failed and others do not want public attention or pity.

However, I can illustrate the process from my own experience. I am not typical as I am outspoken and have challenged the rules and system more publicly than many others. While my attempts to enter the mainstream occurred some time ago, I have no evidence that the situation has changed over the past decade or so in ways that make my experiences irrelevant. There are common elements which seem now to happen all too frequently. The timing of my problems was significant insofar as I fell early, but many women have since suffered the same fate.

I remember during one such time, trying to explain to a then senior woman that it was because I was a feminist and a woman that I was in trouble, not because I was difficult. She and others saw my problems as of my own making. I am amused that today some of those who were part of my problem rewrite history by claiming I chose to work independently, rather than that I was forced to.

As someone who has been in trouble for my interpersonal work skills, I have had to examine the assumptions and practices about female management style. There has been justifiable criticism of my faults in managing others.

I have sometimes behaved in a way generally defined as more male—in leaving to others the details of the process and its management. I can claim that, unlike most males, I did appreciate what was being done and recognised that the tasks required a higher level of skills than I was capable of. I feel that these skills of managing tasks are grossly undervalued.

I recognise the danger in seeing high-level support skills as inferior to other skills. I know I would rather work on drafting policy and undertaking research than manage my own house, or be available to move the office. I am better at policy than moving, but have the greatest respect for those who can move. I realise the problem is the difficulty of valuing skills within continuing masculine based hierarchies.

I accept that my behaviour has sometimes hurt the women with whom I worked. However, I wonder about the strength of their reactions. Had I not been a feminist, or a woman, would the reactions have been so strong? I am concerned that the judgments made of me were very different from those applied to men. Would a man have the same expectations made of him regarding the way he handled some of the decisions or the details of his job? Was I being damned for being unfeminine?

Women like me find difficulties in being what we are: good at some of the skills which are uncommon for women, and not so good at others deemed as womanly. I am difficult to work with, sometimes. I talk fast, think fast and am often demanding. I am outcome oriented and less aware of process, though usually I am prepared to accept direction on this. I take risks and think laterally and often come up with too many ideas, too many for me and anyone else to undertake and often these are too new for others to be comfortable with.

I can name my faults but I find it much harder to name my strengths, and I tend to undervalue them when they seem unwomanly. I nurture others, provide immense support and have encouraged many women who have worked for me to have a go, to move on to new and exciting jobs or study. There are many more achievements and strengths that I could list but I feel these are often obscured by my perceived status as a difficult woman.

If the anger I and other women arouse is disproportionately severe because we do not conform to acceptable female behaviour, there are serious implications for women who aim for positions of leadership. If we restrict female models to feminine ones, we are asking for trouble. We cannot offer any single form of leadership as there are many ways in which women would lead, probably as many as the methods men use.

Some years ago I was the director of a community organisation, with staff problems. One day when I was being criticised by another staff member for failing to attend a meeting, I asked why my deputy was not subjected to similar criticism when she did not make it. The staff member looked at me and said, 'Oh, we feel sorry for her . . . ' She stopped, then said, 'You're right, it is not fair, but you're strong so we expect you to be perfect'.

This stuck in my memory because it indicates the forms of behaviour that women can get away with. Women can gain support by being victims, by showing weaknesses and distress. But those women who find this uncomfortable have difficulty when we come across as strong. This sets up for us the dilemma of being neither acceptably 'female' in style, nor being male and therefore acceptably strong.

I remember a few years later working for a very choleric senior public servant, whose frequent red-faced outbursts of temper were tolerated by the women on his support staff. They saw his reaction as a reasonable response to the stress under which he, and the rest of us, worked. I also remember the trouble I copped the one time I lost my temper; there were no allowances made for my stress levels.

This episode was one in a series which resulted in my losing a senior policy position in the New South Wales Public Service. I was rolled on just such complaints, made initially by a staff member who bitterly resented a decision I had made which countered one she had taken. The fact that the complaint came from a woman and there were others from another couple of women was the seemingly legitimate catalyst the men at the top needed. They could be seen as defenders of the feminine and removers of a woman who failed what they saw as good female management criteria.

This started a process which eventually led to my resignation from the public service. The accusations concerned my management style but no details were ever provided, so I could not defend myself. The reputation stuck and made it almost impossible for me to be considered for other senior jobs. This was despite recognition of my broad knowledge and competence at developing policies, and a range of staff more than willing to work with me.

When I failed in attempts to secure senior jobs, women friends pointed out that I was difficult and obviously not suited to these positions. When I was rolled out of a senior job, they explained that I was just not suited to the public sector. When I was apparently blackballed and couldn't find another job I was again reminded I was difficult.

Even applying for femocrat jobs at the time was not an option. I was rolled from these by senior women. Presumably they were anxious that I was a possible loose cannon and therefore they did not want to take risks with what would be visible controversial positions. I suspect that senior women are often less likely to take risks with their appointments of femocrats now than were the men who first appointed them.

It may, therefore, become increasingly hard for women who are labelled as difficult, or even outspoken, to find jobs at senior and influential levels. Sadly, I suspect this is more so in areas where these traits may be assets to the change process.

What happens to difficult women? After some time, I certainly fulfilled the description. I was angry at seeing both other women and men with fewer skills and competence survive and prosper. I believed that I must have some major personal flaw which made me unable to work in a normal setting.

This seriously undermined my self-confidence and I had a very tough time trying to find alternative ways of using my skills. I set up an explicitly feminist consultancy, not from home like other women, but in an office with staff. If no one else would have me, I would start my own organisation. I also thought that maybe those who knew of my skills would feel more comfortable using my firm than employing me on their staff.

For four years I worked with a group of women and we did some fantastic work. My hopes of forming a network of other feminist consultants failed to eventuate, for many of the reasons I explore in this book. Similarly, the support from feminists in the system was patchy and not commensurate with my professional skills or what we could offer. We worked hard and produced a range of good research and reports which raised many issues that would otherwise have been overlooked.

At the same time, there were assumptions from the women in the system and the community that I would continue to offer a free service of advocacy, advice and support for other women. The pro bono component cost us time and money and was not balanced by what I would consider appropriate and fair access to some of the better paid consultancies in my areas of expertise. I was, after all, a difficult woman.

We tread a slippery path. I have used a few examples here, amongst the many I have experienced or observed. There are many women who have been judged, and damned as failures, on criteria which I believe are harder and narrower than those applied to men for equivalent behaviour.

## CHAPTER 8

# Ortho-doxies
## – Women as Peers

The question of why women are so hard on other women has not received as much attention as our problems with men. I suggest it goes back to the more restricted images with which we have to comply. We need to ask how women cope with women outside the roles of mother and sister, and maybe daughter. Not very well, is the conclusion of my reading and experiences. What we have not yet identified are the problems women face both within peer groups and in recognising other women as possible leaders.

Women have relatively limited experience of dealing with female peers. The emphasis in the 1970s on sisterhood is now a relic of a more optimistic movement, and a somewhat naive one as the reality of differences between women made it impossible. The term *sister* has been relegated to a period of history but the issues it raised are still with us.

The socialisation of women combined with some of the feminist rhetoric suggested that women should be good, supportive and sisterly, sometimes in need of help and nurture, at other times able to offer those to others. The reality is that these qualities are restrictive and relate to a social control process we use in families to get compliance from children and spouses.

In their early years at school, some small girls can already be pinpointed as perpetual outsiders. We can also see the power brokers at this young age, the little girls already adept at creating relationships and hierarchies by bestowing and withdrawing favours, and we see the pain they cause.

One of our problems is that in childhood we did not have the same amount of training offered boys of working in larger groups, of taking the lead or learning to be part of a cooperative team. Sport and action games include these aspects of learning, while doll play and intense friendships make for different lessons.

The socialisation of girls, as nurturers and carers, does not leave much space for the development of relationships or support from their peer groups. Boys are encouraged into teams and gangs, and working together is emphasised in their socialisation. They are geared to competition, aggression and success, and at the same time they are made aware of the need to develop peer support and 'mateship'.

The military model, which essentially transferred into the 'command' workplace models, is about hierarchies, taking and giving orders. However, it is also about the process of working in squads and units, that is, relying on others on your level as well.

Girls can also share and be in gangs, but within these groups they still tend to allocate favours on the basis of being 'best friends'. By the adolescent years the edge becomes individualised as popularity with others and social success become the goals. Some girls in sporting teams follow more of a peer model, but this is again based on the male, militaristic style which is at odds with female socialisation.

It seems that women in groups—whether these are the formal community organisations in which we predominate, the specific women's groups, or the more radical collectives—often have difficulty with peer relationships. The early sisterhood emphasis was a powerful image of links that did not involve the more unequal, more common images of mother or daughter.

Moving women into leadership roles raises the need for followers and for peer relationships. Some of the issues that make it difficult for those who move out front are partly the result of problems women have in relating to their peers. Leadership requires the ability to work in groups, to work with peers, to move from the peer group with its support, and to be able to work with others. It is a two-way process by which the group and its members validate the people who try to move on and move the group with them.

The issue of whether or not leadership is a role for one person working alone is examined in the last section of this book. It may be possible to devise alternate models which make the process less macho and isolating. However, ideally these will spring from the group processes in which women take part.

## Sissies or sisterhood

Men find groups of women uncomfortable. When I have run workshops for women in many different workplaces, there is constant reporting of hostile responses from men, not only because they are excluded, but because women together are seen as threatening. There are comments about the 'sisterhood', the term implying some underhand purpose, some Mafia-style conspiracy.

The words *gossip, chatter, babble* and *bitch* are all applied to communication between women. They imply that the discourses are at best trivial and, at worst, destructive. This is why there is little encouragement for women to group, to develop their own forms of peer interaction. It is recognised, certainly in the Australian context, that men need their mates and the pub/club/footy culture is part of this. Women's needs are seen as being satisfied by home and family, and maybe a friend or two.

Jane Mills, in her account in *Womanwords*[1] of the many ways in which language is used to define us, points out that the term *sisterhood* is often used negatively though *brotherhood* usually has a positive and strong meaning. She shows that the use of the term as a condemnation is not new.

There are further examples in the *Oxford English Dictionary*: 'the shrieking sisterhood' was used in 1873 to describe the women reformers, and by 1910 it had degenerated to mean 'female busybodies' (are there ever male ones?). By this time the suffragist terms were also being undermined.

Sisters who serve others, like nuns and nurses, are seen as admirable, but those focusing on their own needs as women are not. This devaluing of women's groups, designed to isolate women and compel us to relate to men and not each other, is a common process. As a reaction to this the slogan 'Sisterhood is Powerful' was adopted in 1968 by the newly reinvented women's liberation movement in the USA, as well as in Australia and the UK. By highlighting the solidarity of women we hoped to undermine the idea that women could not group.

We did not recognise the need for work to be done to

establish better peer relationships amongst women. One aspect of this work was to identify the process of isolation which divided us. This was an important basis for establishing the consciousness-raising groups that were around in the first few years of the second wave. Working together and developing trust were very much part of the early feminist groups, including the Women's Electoral Lobby. Many of the bonds made then still hold today as a measure of trust and mutual respect.

We argued in the early days that the personal was political, meaning that our issues and concerns were outside the current definitions of what was political. Because we worked in collectives and were aware of the growing power of women, we assumed this would translate into alternative ways of operating in peer groups. I often quip that we seem now to have moved the political to the personal, and individuals and groups spend much of their time disapproving of the way other women work, dissipating political anger on them.

Women have few models to emulate, except male ones. Then we have to face the disparagement women's imitations may attract. As well, groups of women working together always raises the shadow of 'special friendships', that is, sexual relationships between women. So the issue of conforming heterosexuality becomes part of the process which controls the behaviour of women.

Similarly, the ridicule shown to men associating with women, or adopting women's ways, exacerbates the problems for all those who feel that the present methods of dealing with structures are unsatisfactory. Men label other men as 'sissies', which further undermines the possible strength of sisters and sisterhood.

We need to remember that there are no words that denote strength for women which have fully positive meanings. Strong women may be seen as viragos, battle-axes or, at best, Amazons, a word which has both positive and negative connotations. This means that there is a gap in the conceptual rulers we use to measure ourselves.[2]

Women in leadership are only generally acceptable in the broad community when men are absent. A woman competing with men on their terms has another set of problems to face. When both men and women are in leadership roles, it is often assumed that women should not be like men, but be comple- mentary to them. This brings us back to assumptions about gender that may have some utility in short-term EEO debates, and as part of the rationale for encouraging women to enter senior positions, but which can have very deep pitfalls.

## Feminist management may be awful too

Is there a feminine or even feminist style of management which can be generalised as an alternative to the current models? I want to look at some of the presumptions about what constitute female management skills and the way they become part of the prob- lems women create amongst and for ourselves.

If women are deemed bad managers, is it because we have failed a male model of management, or because we practised it? What happens if we fail the approved female or feminist definitions of good managers? We have to examine these definitions and make sure we are not offering a new but equally narrow set of stereotypes. We must ensure that what is labelled as feminist management actually stands up as good management practice. Many of the services run for and by women have attempted to implement various ways of managing through non-hierarchical and participatory structures, and some of these concepts are seen as examples of feminist management.

I suggest that much of what we expect of women as leaders and managers today creates some unintended and unfortunate consequences. Women have been able to attack other women's management styles secure in the fact they are supporting the best feminist practices.

## Correctives and collectives

The early days of feminism saw considerable debate on structures. The consciousness-raising groups, which helped women within the movement to bond, took from many of the 1960s debates a radical, anarchic form. The basis of this was equality of power within the group; a flattened structure which shared skills, tasks and power.

This was a reaction to the rigid, hierarchical structures of existing male left-wing groups, which had often been our entry point to politics. Many of us had cut our political teeth in the anti-Vietnam War movement or other peace groups and had no desire to follow the stacking and counter-stacking that often created rifts and splits in these movements. We were going to be different, and collectives became the basis for the difference. We all sat in circles, avoiding any structures or rules which would inhibit the goal of achieving genuinely consensual decisions. It often worked because in those days we were relatively few and the consciousness raising, coupled with delighted recognition that others thought like us, created deep bonds.

We were happy that we had found a model which abolished hierarchies and made us all equal. We made collectives and lack of structure a basic tenet of feminism. We abolished positions of leadership and developed ways to share responsibility and control.

What I remember of this in practical terms was trying to make Gestetner machines print and somehow always ending up inky. The philosophy of the collective process was that if we shared all tasks and skills, we could all learn to do everything and therefore avoid power plays.

This was a concept that came under scrutiny fairly early in the piece. I remember reading an article from an early issue of *Ms Magazine*[3] called 'The Tyranny of Structurelessness' by Jo Freeman. Copies of it were handed around at meetings and it was discussed almost as a heresy, but one which echoed some of our doubts.

In this article, Freeman identified the way that lack of rules and formal procedures could allow those with leadership tendencies or dominance skills to take over. This would involve more dangerous and unaccountable forms of dominance over informal groups; with no rules there were no controls on the powerful. She signalled the possible dangers of those with experience and confidence being able to take control and thereby use informal structures to wield power. This experience in the early

1970s made us more careful about the collective process but it didn't discourage us from believing that this was still the way to go.

Many of the growing number of women's services offering refuge and support used the collective as a model for their management. This created problems as funding from government often required formal accountability and corporate structures. Nevertheless, the services managed to maintain a fair degree of collectivity by organising the workers and having the formal board as a cipher.

Some of these collectives operated for a long time. The Refractory Girl collective of which I was a member, worked effectively for over twenty years to produce a quarterly feminist journal. We were successful mainly because we were always very task focused.

Collectives seem to stumble when there is conflict and it becomes personal. Generally women find conflict hard to deal with, so the issue of how people feel, the interpersonal dynamics and the lack of structures can create real problems. The push for consensus presents a further difficulty as it is slow and fails in some of its premises. The theory of consensus assumes that those seeking the answers have common ground and are sufficiently comfortable with each other to be able to explore options before reaching an outcome. In practice, it often becomes a process of endurance and emotional bullying designed to achieve agreement rather than explore the best options. Similarly, some theories of conflict resolution assume that there is always a win/ win option. Both these models ignore the many situations where there are genuine and maybe irreconcilable differences on issues and also a variety of informal (and maybe formal) power levels.

Combine this with the dynamics of a group and the particular reactions of most women to conflict, and the mixture is potentially explosive. The problems endemic to group processes have been solidly documented and include: creating ingroups and outgroups; rewarding conformity; withdrawing approval; isolating outsiders; creating a scapegoat to achieve cohesion for others; or developing factions.

While these can appear in most organisations, the lack of structure in collectives makes it easier for informal conformity and scapegoating to occur. Many women I have talked to have found collective meetings quite painful and stressful. The lack of rules means that those unhappy with what goes on are theoretically free to raise their concerns, but are then often labelled as difficult or troublemakers.

I have seen this happen in other groups for which I have acted as facilitator. Participants in training groups of women, for example, often acknowledge that they feel deeply uncomfortable with their inability to deal with conflict. I have counselled and supported women who have found themselves, as I did, constructed as the outsider or the scapegoat. This meant they were denied a sense of emotional belonging to the group. For women, socialised to maintain relationships and be validated by them, this can be devastating.

There is some truth in the image of the woman who uses her skills in relationships to cause pain. The intensity and importance placed on relationships gives women the capacity to create a considerable power bloc. As an observer and participant in many different groups which would call themselves feminist, I suggest that those women who bond most closely are also likely to exclude and punish others by using emotional techniques.

Women in collectives often reproduce the modes of behaviour they bring from their families. These may be useful but may also involve forms of victim play and emotional blackmail that are part of the power of being powerless. In my experience they would seem to lead to collectives continuing to reproduce themselves over time by hiring only those who fit in. In this way they become almost mirror images of the processes that occur in the boardroom. This does not mean there is no diversity; most collectives aim for a balance of identified groups. However, those who make it most successfully are those who fit in.

## Doing over the leader

Leadership implies followers and many women who have tried to lead have found themselves with no one behind. The front runner, looking back for the rest of the field, sees no one in sight and wonders if she has gone the wrong way. For some women the experience of being in front feels the same as being an outsider.

The orthodoxy of women's groups outlined above sets collective decision making into the culture of the organisation. If decisions become too hard and lead to conflict, the organisation moves into a process of group maintenance.

Many women's groups are set up for support and consensus building, and being different is only acceptable if the difference is of disadvantage. The model of good womanly behaviour is to be one amongst the group and not to stand out. If you need assistance to aspire to the group standard, you are acceptable. If you are a person with ideas and what, in masculine terms, are defined as leadership qualities you may often find yourself being isolated as difficult.

My experiences in various roles have shown me the folly of trying to move too far out in front. The day I started writing this chapter, I was feeling very angry as I cleared the last remnants of my feminist consultancy. This was not just a woman working in her spare bedroom, but a complete, upfront office with a range of women's groups with few resources amongst the tenants, a big pro bono demand and the potential to do some really good research and training.

Again, I realised that I had outrun my peers, moved too fast and been punished for it. I pick up publications that now say what I was saying many years ago, when other women thought I was too far outside what someone described recently as 'the loop'. This is the area of accepted thinking, of ideas which have the comfort of familiarity, where the major tasks are reinforcing each other, not innovation.

Groups of women are very good at supporting those who conform, but find it harder to support those who do not. This is not simply our fault as we are working from a position of relative powerlessness and defensiveness within society. The problem is that the barriers these processes set up for those who do not fit can be powerful and destructive. Within groups some women act as moral guardians, sometimes inadvertently working against their avowed intentions by limiting members' freedom to move.

One woman involved in a feminist group which had a strong and demanding ethos of sameness, described her way of dealing with this as saving up her green stamps. If she was quiet, supportive, polite and compliant for some time, she was allowed a brief spurt of public leading and anger. The sad part of her story was that it was other women who measured out the control. We need to examine whether there are aspects of inherited, albeit socially derived, women's cultures that inhibit women's performance as change agents.

This is the point at which we should remember the role of God's police which women tend to fill, often by choice. The tag used by Caroline Chisholm[4] last century to justify bringing out free women immigrants to 'control' men was echoed in the suffrage battles, when women were seen as more likely to vote for increased social control and temperance.

There are still overtly policing women's groups, such as those on the moral right. Even though they are there to protect women, and control men, they sometimes find common ground with the more puritanical feminist groups, but these are not issues for this book.

If women's groups are to offer an alternative view of both content and process, we need to examine whether the modes we work within, either the more structured and traditional ones, or the less structured collectives, offer us the necessary training grounds for leadership.

The examples above do not undermine my case that women need to be leaders. They simply show that women are not saints nor necessarily wise. Women are moving from positions of oppression that leave scars and create forms of resistance which are less than admirable, and are ultimately not transferable to leadership positions.

The possible movement of women into leadership roles is therefore likely to be stunted unless we can change these aspects of the culture of femininity and women's groups. This is within our power and can be done both before and during our attempts to change the main organisations in our society which are still dominated by men. We need also to look at the lessons we can learn in practising new ideas within women's groups and organisations, and explore how we could and should do things differently and what we need to retain.

## Detribalising and dissent

The models of informal collectives for women's groups were based on an assumed tribal format, the older form of community where we were bound by the links of family and society. This is also the model often described as indigenous, where group identification is strong and demands allegiance. As well, it is used by groups confronting a threat or form of oppression which require cohesion for survival. It is the way those who sense their weakness or vulnerability create a place for self-protection and mutual support.

In the theories of society, this model is called structuralist. The social units discipline their members and allocate prescribed roles. Change and conflict are seen as pathologies which threaten the whole and therefore must be controlled or expunged. This sometimes works in new movements and with small numbers of people. It is also a useful model for those societies where charismatic leaders want total adherence to their ideas; creating control over a large group. Religions often use this model, and those demanding fundamental adherence to beliefs find the combination of a sense of belonging and sanctions very effective.

The past decade has seen much more evidence of aggression within and between small groups where two blocs faced each other than there has been in the previous years of the postwar period. The new tribes are based on ingroup–outgroup processes which may sometimes end in civil wars.

While this is not necessarily the end result of tribal forms, it sends up a warning signal that processes of belonging should not seek to exclude and create ingroups through their enmity to outgroups. Many of the conflicts I see within women's groups, and between them, have elements of this process. This is because they rely on the emotive belonging, rather than on a more rational process of debate and agreement.

This does not mean I am advocating we accept the masculine forms of warrior formations where leadership is often a product of hazing and violence. This is also a form of tribal cohesion based on hierarchy and obedience to power. Neither of these forms works well. In the social system I am envisaging, neither war nor gender oppression would be acceptable.

Can we provide a model that allows us to innovate and create and still be seen as part of the group, rather than being an outsider and pariah?

CHAPTER 9

# Where are the
# Heroines?

We need heroines. Images of strong women help us to see ourselves as strong. Both men and women use the web of images, beliefs and ways of being, to provide us with a sense of who we are. Where no images or models exist we have difficulty inventing ourselves. Our history and culture, expressed both formally and informally, give us ways of being and seeing which can limit or expand the way we perceive ourselves.

The problems raised in the previous chapters have not just developed amongst women today. They reflect the limited and often relatively powerless images of women that have always surrounded us, and impress upon us the constraints of femininity. The women's movement, for all its achievements, has not yet produced sufficient counter-images to allow us to be confident of some of the alternatives, and in particular of proclaiming them from a position of strength.

The pantheons of modern times from the seventeenth century contain few women. Earlier periods are probably best examined through the various religious and mythological tracts we have available. Myths are both symbols and normative structures: they represent what was once seen and believed but are also able to be reinterpreted as times change. Therefore, the roles of women and particularly of powerful women in myths can provide interesting insights.

It is useful for us to re-examine and rewrite both the distant and recent past to include women. In some cases, this seems to require considerable rejigging to create a mythic past in which women were dominant, and to look for evidence of the great patriarchal war when, presumably, men took over. This should be seen as part of the process of making the myths we need in order to see ourselves as powerful. Despite this, I have personal problems with accepting the vogue for goddesses and witchcraft as I have with the more recent male godheads.

I grew up with the Graeco/Roman myths, which were stories offering possible images of womanhood. The gods and goddesses were all too human in their relationships and problems: Hera (Juno), Aphrodite (Venus), Athena (Minerva), Artemis (Diana) and Demeter (Ceres) provide interesting archetypes. Hera, wife of Zeus, was the first example of referred and betrayed power. Venus was always in trouble, because of the conjunction of love and beauty; Athena was the goddess of wisdom and handicrafts, but was also a warrior and known for killing giants; and Artemis was interested in what might have been regarded as male areas, such as hunting.

Are they our heroines? I don't think so, and it is a comment on the paucity of images of strong women that we have to go back to the ancients to get any images at all. Some women, in search of metaphors through the Greek myths, make the point that these goddesses were patriarchal victims. This is not the image I retain. From my early readings, they appeared to have fun and power, and their trouble came from their actions, not from being victims.

The Bible gives us a few women to admire. Some stand out as heroines: Ruth and Naomi were very feminine in their achievements of friendship; my namesake Eve was just trouble; and Mary was a pure vessel rather than an active participant. There was Judith who killed an evil general Holofernes, and Delilah who was the embodiment of betrayal. In western religions there is a range of saints but these, both male and female, are generally sufferers rather than activists.

Women occur in other religious myths, such as Kali and her Hindu peers who perhaps represent some models of Hindu activism. There were Taoist women now lost from view. However in all cases we return to distant myths, often from religions no longer practised, or which have changed so completely that they are no longer useful.

Overall we are denied the models of strong heroines. Despite this, there are always some women who make it as leaders and politicians. Some are acceptable, 'almost as good as a man' versions of women. Some started in more conventional ways by replacing a family member or husband who formerly held a leadership position. Her role was to carry on his; to replicate his leadership characteristics. These women have provided the bulk of the women leaders in the international sphere. Some went on to become powerful in their own right, such as Indira Gandhi (Nehru's daughter), Mrs Bandaranaike in Sri Lanka, Corazon Aquino, and Benazir Bhutto.

There are a few leaders who could be deemed feminist. Mary Robinson, the Irish President whose role is mainly ceremonial, has made her mark. Gro Brundtland, Prime Minister of Norway has many women in her Cabinet, and Joan Kirner and Carmen Lawrence had brief glory as Premiers in Australia.

## Cross-dressing and passing

Women lack models of strength and power; strong women who have led change and created leadership roles. So, probably like many other girls, I remember when I was little wanting to be a boy because boys had adventures.

If you couldn't be a boy, a tomboy might do; George in *The Famous Five*, Jo in *Little Women*, for instance, who were named after boys and determined to show pluck. The *Girls' Own Annuals* of the 1930s and 1940s carried stories of girls who were naughty and non-conformist and sought action rather than soppy 'girl behaviour', and I lapped this up. Now when I look back, I realise they were mirroring male behaviour within acceptable limits.

There were scant possibilities for the anglophone child. Christopher Robin, Winnie the Pooh and friends were almost indubitably male, as were Thomas the Tank Engine and most of his friends. Becky Thatcher in *Tom Sawyer* just got lost while Tom and Huckleberry Finn had adventures. The Little Mermaid was a victim who dies in the end (although the recent Disney film has a happy ending in which she lives); the Cinderella legend had ugly sisters in the assertive roles; and there were many strong bad women as witches or wicked stepmothers who persecuted the good but wimpish central characters.

Becky Sharp in *Vanity Fair* was a bitch, and most of the classics we read offered passionate women but rarely leaders. Jane Austen modelled wit, but the Brontës modelled doom. I can remember my frustration as heroines became hopeless, unable to act, needing to be rescued; or were defeated by love. Therefore, it is not surprising that I saw males as more appropriate models and through adolescence held the idea that women were rather dull.

Surrounding girls with powerful images of men and weak ones of women is part of the process of identification that we face; power is Other and dependence is Self. I read many boys' books, looking for action and for characters who seemed to have some control over what happened and some effect on the outcomes.

For boys, the process is reversed as the screen and page offer images of manhood which demand instant identification and adherence to a hero model. The schooldays stories for both boys and girls, often set in English boarding schools, saw the images of leaders as limited indeed and the non-conformists were often also the scapegoats.

The message for me was that in order to be able to *do* anything one had to be a boy or near boy. Being a girl was a bore. I have informally checked this with many of my peers, albeit mostly from the pre-TV generation, and had similar reports. It is interesting to speculate what might have happened to those who grew up on the 'Brady Bunch' and Barbie dolls.

I used to fantasise about having a male twin. Shakespeare produced some good examples, such as Viola and Sebastian, which suggested to me that cross-dressing had some possibilities. Portia in *The Merchant of Venice* made me want to be a lawyer, but none of them offered the woman a role as a cross-dressed leader.

We identify children by gender at a very young age. There is evidence that if you give an adult a cross-dressed baby (that is, a girl in blue clothes or vice versa) the adult will respond to the signalled gender; cooing and cuddling with the pink dressed boys, and rough-housing the blue dressed girls.

The early assumption of gender in a child is relatively recent. This is outlined in the Introduction to *Vested Interests*,[1] a book on cross-dressing and cultural anxieties by Marjorie Garber. The author notes that the garb of all small children in the West was very 'feminine' until well into the twentieth century. Prior to World War I pink was the colour of choice for boys and blue for girls. This was finally switched as late as the end of World War II.

There have been a number of documented cases of women cross-dressing to achieve the status of men, using male dress to gain access to work, for safety, and prestige.

Referring again to the examples found in children's literature, in some female and even male stories, girls who became plucky little surrogate males, were accepted as boys, and if cross-dressed could 'pass' as male. In contrast, the sissy, sensitive, artistic, non-powerful male was unacceptable to males or females. His was the greater betrayal because in rejecting or failing the test of manhood he slipped closer to the Other.

Passing is an interesting phenomenon. It is best observed in the writings on race where the western, white view invoked the idea that most non-whites would naturally seek to pass as white. After all, being just like a white man was considered praise indeed for the 'native' henchmen who assisted white heroes.

Passing as a sanctioned way of joining the majority is an assimilation model, used in Australia for 'civilising' Aboriginal children who were removed from their parents so that they could be trained in white ways. When they were light skinned the children were often adopted by whites so they could leave their purported inferior status behind. This was an attempt to destroy the value of their existing cultures and therefore their sense of self. There were also those who chose to pass so they could get jobs or housing or even entry into the swimming pool. Passing was an affirmation of the superiority of the group to which one was aspiring. Passing as black is an illogical concept, and whites who 'went native' were despised and rejected. The process reinforces social status and reflects power relationships.

Passing as male, if female, is often reported in literature and history where it was seen as reasonable as long as it was not a sign of 'deviant' sexuality. Women who cross-dressed so they could become doctors, join the army or be the 'man' in economic or professional ways, were met with ambivalent reactions but often with some admiration. Their aspiration to male status and power was understandable. But the reverse of males wanting female status was seen by men, at least, as bizarre and more often as a betrayal of the tenets of masculinity.

The significance of the process of passing is that it undermines the identity of the group who have to do it. Being a coconut (black outside, white inside) is a description of shame for Aborigines as it degrades their own culture and their sense of self. While women obviously share the cultures of their male peers and their class positions, they also have the problems of negotiating a version of being as legitimate as men's.

One of the seminal writers in this area was Frantz Fanon, a black psychiatrist from one of the French colonies, post World War II. He had a particular interest in concepts of identity. In his book *Black Faces, White Masks*[2] Fanton outlined the concept of 'negritude': the great difficultly that educated, colonised blacks had in maintaining their sense of a non-white identity.

The 'white mask' was their French educated identity, which made them hollow men belonging to neither culture and denying what their own had to offer. This process of colonisation created the sense of living as Others, of being defined in terms set by those with more power, whose approval is sought subconsciously. In this process your sense of self becomes a sense of otherness.

Simone de Beauvoir formulated a similar framework for women in her 1949 book *The Second Sex*.[3] She wrote that women are defined by their sense of being for others. We see ourselves primarily through the eyes of others—we are wives and mothers, defined by our relationships to men. It is their criteria which establishes what we are to aspire to and what is valued.

## Dominating the Other

The ideas and actions that are rewarded in any community tend to be set by the groups that run the system. From their tastes and interests come the whole box and dice of social and political culture. The less powerful minorities within those societies often incorporate and internalise the views of the dominant group. They tend to like what the dominant group likes and despise what it dislikes, as a way of identifying with the powerful and also of being rewarded for behaving properly.

This theory of social identification appears in the writings of various disciplines: politics, philosophy, sociology and psychology. In everyday life, we see it in the way people are influenced by images in the media of the rich and famous. In its most obvious manifestation, the fashion and beauty industries, we can see it work on styles and body images.

Problems lie in the way women are perceived and in the judgments then applied to us. This explains in part why women often tend to believe men and not other women and why some women may be more punitive than men themselves. We are lulled into believing that what is male is actually universal and that there are no alternatives. Women are left with the assumption that male qualities are more desirable than female ones, and that being female involves reflection of power, never its possession. Aspiring to masculine qualities is only allowable if no male is there to offer his services, or if women join an almost androgynous, neutral group like the spinster professionals of old. In looking at these examples, we can begin to identify why women become supporters of the status quo. We have no separate space, no area of culture that we can claim as ours. Nevertheless, the organisation of gender roles allocates to women certain areas defined as women's space, like the household. Women have therefore developed an interdependence with men and vice versa. We reap benefits from the status of the man or suffer with him if his status is limited.

There is the biologistic view that some social scientists and political groups would have us adopt. This synthesis of man and woman creates a unit known as the family, which is deemed to be the unit of society. The International Year of the Family discussion paper[4] calls this unit the smallest democracy, suggesting it reproduces the citizen rights we have outside of the home.

We need to acknowledge that women have had little direct input into the public manifestations of societies. The standards set in law, politics, education and culture have been established by those with the public power, that is, men. This results in women perceiving themselves, and being seen by men, as the Other.

## Desirable women

The images of the acceptable female are likely to reflect the limits set by the dominant culture. Blonde, blue-eyed princesses seem the only model for a wide range of multi-coloured children from anglophone countries, as this is an image from the dominant British Christian culture. Even angels are blue-eyed and blond and only the devil is dark.

Unfortunately women, as well as men, admire these restricted views of beauty because women are also affected by the standards set by the dominant group. Women often actively promote the dominant ideals and reinforce them as part of their secondary identity processes, by which they identify themselves through men. The female ideal of beauty or behaviour is set by males and is not far from the picture of the golden haired, blue-eyed princess. Thus many of the women who do succeed, conform to both a physical and psychological template which is determined by the masculine and feminine acceptance of it.

### Playing like a man!

The behaviour which I have just described occurs throughout our society. Why would a barrister choose to put women on juries when she was defending a man? In theory, it should work against her client, but she knows from experience that women are more prepared to believe men than they are women; the male defendant is seen as more credible than the female victim or witness. There is not as much empathy for the under-dog, the one who resembles the juror.

In fact, disbelieving the female victim or witness' story and siding with the male defendant may provide some immunity to being like the victim. 'Compassion fatigue' is a phenomenon identified by charity collectors when images of horror become too common and lose their power to elicit sympathy. Perhaps there is a similar process which occurs with empathy, when it becomes a threat to one's own sense of power to identify with the victims. This raises a serious question about the legitimacy of the claim that to bring more women into power will lead to change. It can also show that some women will reflect and extend the dominant masculine values and often be more gung-ho about them than many men. So although it is essential to raise the number of women in senior positions, there are other issues that we must address in order to achieve change.

On the TV program 'Sunday',[5] Graham Richardson, ex Labor Senator and powerbroker, expressed his doubts that more women in politics would improve the overall quality of politicians. He based his beliefs on three criteria:

1. The women in politics had made no real difference yet;
2. If quotas were imposed better men would have to be 'sacrificed' to make space for less able women;
3. The women would not have been 'blooded' by attending thousands of dreary meetings and all the other paraphernalia of party politics.

As part of the segment on this influential current affairs program, Richardson invited responses from three very competent women politicians. Democrat Senator Cheryl Kernot made the statement that equality meant both mediocre male and female politicians but that currently women were expected to be super females. Federal Labor Minister Carmen Lawrence voiced her plea for permission to climb down from the pedestal on which she has been placed which makes her particularly vulnerable to falling. Opposition Senator Amanda Vanstone gave the example of how her input was used but her contributions not acknowledged because men took the limelight.

In his conclusions, Richardson ignored or discounted most of what they said. He believes that the system in place should not be questioned and that current criteria should still be used. His theory encapsulates many of the problems experienced by women as it ignores the masculine biases both in the ideas and the structures that support them.

The problem of encouraging more women into politics was set

up in Richardson's argument as women displacing men. This is a conflict model which is alien to most women and therefore likely to be rejected.

The process of entry into politics through the branches, with all the time-wasting and rituals this entails was seen by Richardson as a rite of passage and without it women were not entitled to the post. This is despite the fact that there is no evidence that this local level cockfighting actually prepares potential politicians for more than thuggery and a capacity to count the numbers.

The three female politicians believed that in reality the criteria for women succeeding were different from those for men, as they had to be better than just passable. This meant women would be more likely to fail.

These politicians also found that when women did do something worth noticing, it was often the men who took credit. This is an issue I receive constant feedback on in workshops: a woman puts up ideas which are then claimed by men, and implemented, without the woman's input or even any recognition that it was her idea.

Women in politics or other leading positions will find they have to respond to criteria set by men, often for men. If they raise issues for women, they will probably have to make these issues acceptable to their male colleagues. And therein lies the tale: even when women make it in these areas, they are forced to comply with masculine rules. We have not yet succeeded in redrawing too many of these and so we are, in Simone de Beauvoir's terms, being for others; defined in their terms; and valued by their criteria.

Are we being male-defined women or surrogate men? Is it the choice between putting on a male mask and playing it by the rules men wrote for themselves, or being women only as defined by masculine values? These questions are confusing and I have deliberately included some of the contradictions. If we assume that there is logic in the present system and any real coherence, we will fail to make changes.

We must assume that the system will confuse us, but we should not assume that this means we have got it wrong. Developing strategies for more female leadership and change requires that we clarify what we want and thereby take some control.

## CHAPTER 10

# Factoring in the
# Feminine

This chapter looks at ways in which the expectations placed on women can lead to our inability to support other women. Influences range from the so-called 'advantages' of femininity, the training of victims, and the effect of too much time at home. These all contribute to the way we see ourselves and other women.

We need to break this nexus by renouncing both the privileges of being protected and the victim status, which may derive from distorted protective measures. We must recognise that in giving up our assumed right to be supported, we also change the nature of our relationships all round. Protective custody may provide security but is also a place of restriction where power cannot co-reside. We need to abrogate one to assume the other. This is not a new problem, nor is its identification. In 1949, Simone de Beauvoir wrote:

*To decline to be the Other, to refuse to be a party to the deal—this would be for women to renounce all the advantages conferred upon them by their alliance with the superior caste. Man-the-sovereign will provide women-the-liege with material protection and will undertake the moral justification of her existence; thus she can evade at once both the economic risk and the metaphysical risk of a liberty in which ends and aims must be contrived without assistance.*[1]

## Dependency and protection—the tyranny of victim

There has been considerable coverage in the media, mainly from the USA, of what I term 'victim feminism'. Allied with the so-called culture of complaint[2] and political correctness, the media and some writers depict feminism as full of woes and ready to truncate free speech. It is true that some of the current feminist material portrays women as always in powerless or victim positions—such as in situations of domestic violence and sexual assault—and sees women as being always exploited and always inferior. This depiction is sometimes used to gain public resources for services to women and is only part of the process which emphasises that survivor is a more appropriate description than victim.

Some women accept that the dependency and protection model is one which offers them certain advantages. These may also be read as disadvantages as they are often posited on the basis of lesser access to money and power. In this are the seeds of the way women treat other women, as there is little in our experiences or education which encourages us to trust and support other women in positions of power.

I mentioned in the Introduction that my (woman) kindergarten teacher gave boys the more interesting percussion instruments such as cymbals and drums. When I was seven, I remember another example of being excluded because I was female. I took some old toys to a toy exchange as this was still wartime and new items were unavailable. I really wanted a meccano set, but was told that a girl shouldn't ask for one. I went home with a crane truck, the most male toy I was allowed, and a somewhat confused mother.

I knew girls were discriminated against but as I grew older the trade-offs became more obvious: being a girl had some advantages. We were allowed to cry, even if I did not want to, and were not expected to fight physically. Some of these benefits have probably faded since the 1940s but they were clear indicators that there were compensations for being a girl.

Girls (women) did not have to go to war, boys became soldiers; this was a powerful message for children who did not know what peace was. Boys were given the role of both protector and initiator of relationships. This was not a role girls (or perhaps even the boys themselves) wanted; being asked out by boys allowed us to avoid the disappointment of refusal, though we did run the risk of no dates. Boys were supposed to collect the girl and bring her home, and thereby were acknowledged as the more powerful and also deemed the most responsible. Men stood up for women in trains and buses, men waited while women went through doors, and were supposed to protect them from harm.

In a sense, we were trained to see ourselves as goods for buying but we were also taught to make sure we controlled the price. This could be regarded as a part of the process of commodification of women, or of the relationship between men and women. It is also often seen as a degradation of women and part of our oppression. However, the other side is that we had something to trade. It put emphasis on our appearance, our sexual innocence and other aspects of the trade in terms of broad gender relationships. In the narrower social arrangements of young women then, and in mutated forms even now, the trade of favours for meals, entertainment and ongoing financial support is part of the equation.

As a young woman, I was a member of a freewheeling, non-conformist group called the Sydney Push. We spent a lot of time in pubs, rebelling against the fairly boring and straitlaced lifestyle of the 1950s and early 1960s. Push women were not into using their sex as a trade for marriage, but we certainly used it for drinks. Acquiring a 'captain', a man who would provide drinks, food and, maybe, money for an evening or longer was not uncommon for those who had no jobs and no desire for them.

In the suburbs our peers endlessly debated whether they would do *it* before they were married, or at least engaged, and whether this would ruin their chances of marriage. Marriage then was a meal ticket, the objective for most young women who did not expect to have to do paid work.

I remember at age eighteen, wandering daringly through the back lanes of East Sydney which was then the red light area. There were four of us, two couples, obviously students sightseeing. The prostitutes' cribs, now upmarket town mews, opened onto the street, and those without clients stood in the doors. They called out to us and the terms they used for us indicated where we fitted on their scales. 'Charity molls, why do you give it away?' was the general tone of the comments. We tend too often to ignore that women have the capacity to use their bodies for trade, an option less commonly available to men.

So what? Who wants the power to whore? It is referred to as the oldest profession and can easily be translated into some aspects of marriage. After all, we were once chattels passed from the ownership of father to that of husband, unable to control our own property or to vote. Giving up our right to be supported when we choose not to earn a wage, may be to our advantage. Servicing another adult full time and unpaid does not create a sense of autonomous power or self-respect.

We need to move away from the assumption that we are owed something for being a woman, that our bodies and service skills are a passport to support. In discussions of censorship and the effects of pornographic films on impressionable minds, I often claim that we should ban *Pretty Woman*. This reworking of the Cinderella fairy tale is just another endorsement that the body beautiful will get you what you want. In this version, the fact that the female character is a 'rescued' hooker makes it even more dishonest. Romance obscures the never-ending story that women can trade their bodies for security.

I remember in my scatty youth being aware that, as a last resort, I could always raise money on my body. I never traded sex for cash, but often meals and sometimes money in the expectation I would offer it. In that way, many sex workers would see their trade as being an upfront and open use of skills and bodies. The household deals often implicit and driven by gender assumptions can create very difficult relationships of privilege and at the same time a sense of powerlessness.

We have not entirely moved from the position of kept women. After all, the word hussy is a derivative of housewife. As the worse aspects of our inferior legal status have been removed, we have retained some of the privileges. There are still many women who believe that they should have the sole right to decide whether they will join the paid work force after marriage and child rearing. This is presumably based on some assumption of trading services such as sex, household chores and child-rearing skills for support. The question is whether the resultant financial dependency is reinforcing a pattern of relationships that becomes a trap.

## Exploring the compliance

One of the phenomena noted above is the way that those who are subservient often absorb the values of the oppressor. French theorists claim that the position of majorities dominating minorities has moved into a politics of difference which sees little space for coalitions or for collective action. It is about power and the way in which the powerful not only run things but speak for the powerless. They proscribe how we are supposed to think and feel as well as act.

There are two major aspects of the way women act which interfere with our attempts to find comfortable images of leadership. Because current leadership models have been defined by and for men it can be difficult for women to have any sense of relevance. This is why it is important to look at the way we both define ourselves, and are defined as Other. The possibilities for women tend to be limited so that we either succeed on the current terms or we fail. There is no third option which would involve actively changing the forms.

As a sociologist, I am looking for ways of explaining the very stubborn resistance to changes in gender relations. There are logical and rational changes to be made for the benefit of all but many of these are not considered or have not been implemented. I realise that change is itself a problem and may involve obvious short-term, and even medium-term, discomforts. However, these do not sufficiently explain the resistance to change we find in many women. This is not only from conservative women or those who benefit in some way from the present system; it spreads to others who could benefit greatly from reform.

In part it is those women who may gain least who are most likely to support change. These women are generally well edu-cated, have reasonable access to power and have been able to make some use of the present system. Those with few choices and whose lives may be adversely affected by gender are often those most alienated from feminism.

My study of power and the identification of the Other took me back to Max Weber for the third time. He theorised power as being double-ended: for any sustained power relationship there must be some level of compliance, and consent from the victim.[3] This is not necessarily consent freely given but may be the result of fear and coercion, of force and the exertion of power. However, it can only be sustained over a long period if the person in the subordinate position recognises the legitimacy of the superordinate. This means that changes by the subordinate affect the superordinate as well.

Given the particular relationship of men and women who live and work together, there are real possibilities for changing the relationship if women shift their ground. This also requires an examination of the types of behaviour that subordinates develop, particularly in close quarters.

## The victim as expert/manager

I remember conversations at Bondi Beach Public when I was in primary school. The morning comparisons of 'beltings' amongst my class mates gained them status I could not acquire and left my verbal punishment in the shade.

I also recall in the early days of WEL (Women's Electoral Lobby) identifying the 'blood on the floor' model of recounting experience. The emphasis on how awful our experiences were set up a bonus for victims. A third example was a dinner I attended with three other 'ethnics', where we each competed to prove our victim credibility by our accounts of persecution. I sat watching myself do it with a sense of absurdity that this was the way one established one's right to speak. Deep in the heart of this process are the stigmata of the best forms of emotional status symbols.

A similar situation arises in policy arenas where women dealing with violence and sexual violence push for these issues to take precedence over others. Because victims of violence are in immediate danger their needs have an urgency that requests for equality cannot match.

This creates the phenomenon of victim feminism as a by-product, or direct product of the pressure on resources. The more pitiful and frequent your victimisation, the more resources you can lay claim to. These victims become, like casualty and trauma patients, major users of limited resources, leaving little for the preventive action of addressing gender inequalities and the associated violence.

The strategy of presenting someone as a victim extends beyond the casualties of violence. The use of what may be called a passive–aggressive approach by women is probably closely connected to ways of 'managing' dominance. It is a response to being in a powerless position and a way of ensuring that you have some protective power, albeit indirect, by blocking what you do not want rather than asking for what you do want.

When I run groups with women in management positions, one of the exercises we do is to look at ways of exerting influence. We go through the various ways in which power and influence manifests in groups. Then I ask them how many have used 'victim' status to exert influence; as a means to power. The first reaction is usually silence. How can I associate the term *victim* with power? This seems to be an oxymoron, that lovely word which means an apparent contradiction, because victim power is often about control of the process. However, it is indirect and passive resistance, using the current process as it stands rather than assuming power and influence.

I follow up this question with another: 'How often do you get what you want without actively pursuing it? For instance, by blocking other people's suggestions until they come up with one you want?'

Then the penny drops. There are always a few who acknowledge they have done this. After all, it is safer to wait till somebody else raises your ideas so you do not have to take the risks yourself. Your role then is to block unwanted options by constantly pointing out why they won't work.

Another version is the sacrificing worker. I remember a senior woman who used this to devastating effect. She controlled the whole office by constantly being a martyr, that is, by assuming control over everything and then complaining of overload. She had no decision-making power and sought to influence the boss by being seen as a good support person. This involved her sabotaging any competition in the influence stakes by appearing to be the only one producing. By constantly claiming overwork, and discouraging support from those she wanted to cut out, she exerted considerable negative power.

Passive power can be quite destructive for the person who uses it and the place in which it is used. It is often responsible for some of the worst cases of office politics. People resent what they see as destructive forces but often feel unable to tackle the proponent because they have already defined themselves as the powerless victim. If anyone points out what is happening the perpetrators will fly into defence. They often genuinely believe themselves to be powerless and overlooked. They truly feel unappreciated and anxious about their lack of recognition. This becomes more acute because they rarely can claim credit for their achievements, as neither they or the others see their role clearly.

This situation can happen with women in both senior and junior positions. In senior positions, sometimes even in the case of the manager, a woman may not want to be seen as the boss; not make clear what she wants; and she may use indirect means to achieve her ends. Again she may appear always to be overloaded and constantly on the edge of being 'let down' by staff who fail to appreciate the way she works for them.

In all these cases, the 'giving in' comes from the guilt of the presumed perpetrator, who feels it is their fault that the 'victim' has been put upon. The inadequacies of other staff to alleviate the problems raised by the person in the victim role demand they increase efforts to satisfy her often unclear needs and demands. The solution may not satisfy anyone, as the victim has never clearly expressed her desired outcome and cannot claim victory. Also, those who have resolved it feel confused by having reached a solution through a barrage of unspecified resistance. Therefore control rests with the person who holds the victim power. However, the process is passive–aggressive and hidden rather than overt. It often develops as a response to genuine anxieties about being seen as assertive or demanding, and is reinforced by its effectiveness. Winning from the passive position is a feminine and unproductive action we need to lose.

I want to make it clear that I am not blaming the victim in the way that women who are raped are accused of being at fault, or of asking for it. This is one of the most pernicious of cultural mythologies often used to exculpate a genuine aggressor from responsibility for their actions. My interest is in group victim status and the way it can be used by individuals to exculpate themselves from any responsibility for their actions.

An interesting mirror on aspects of this debate comes from sections of what is known as the men's movement. Their main attention-getting strategy is to claim loudly and widely their own powerlessness. And this is where we need to look at the contradictions between concepts of leadership and victim.

## The power of victim status

Naomi Wolf, Camille Paglia, Robert Hughes and many others have identified the culture of complaint and victim as part of the public discourses of our time.[4] What has not been identified is the way victims, as a social rather than an individual phenomenon, can become part of the picture, co-opted and used as a form of power in their own right.

Victims are passive but also often powerful. Try dealing with someone who makes you feel guilty, and who claims you are the source of all their troubles. It is a powerfully powerless position from which to create resistance, but it does not lead to change.

This is complicated so maybe using an example of a woman like this will make it clearer. I will take the case of someone I grew up with, my mother. Her life had been pretty horrendous: at age 24 with a new baby she was deprived of her citizenship, her home and her right to complete a university degree by the Nazis. She had to flee from Austria to England in 1939 with no money and me. She became a refugee who moved from a flat in Vienna to a cottage without electricity in Norfolk. She lasted the war in menial jobs waiting for my father to return from the army so she could get on with her life. Unfortunately the life she was waiting for never materialised. By the time her marriage collapsed she had fixed herself firmly into victim mode. She expected to be victimised by everyone in her life, including her second husband and me. And she received much sympathy for having an ungrateful daughter and a difficult husband.

She was therefore untouched by news of fresh disasters. By assuming the worst and acting accordingly, she was fully prepared for whatever tragedies the world handed out. Although her life by this stage was generally good, she stayed vigilant, maintaining the problem status of myself and my stepfather. Even my return to university to complete a degree, the birth of my daughter, my appearances on radio and TV, and my move into prominence and good jobs were always greeted with negative predictions. I felt that I could not get it right and I remember as an adolescent deciding after various attempts, it was no use trying.

My reason for including this example is not for the sympathy vote, but to explain how I was sensitised to the victim power paradox. I realised early on that I could not win: my role was defined as that of being a failure and my success only ruined the script. I can understand the pressures that made my mother set her defences in place. I also saw how it limited her perception of options and her broader influence.

I have since seen and experienced many more examples of this type of behaviour; some of them in the workplace and in community organisations. I worked in an office once with a very powerful minion who made our boss unable to act on my advice, lest she punished him. Because of her actions I had no access to typing, no place in the office structure, and the frustration of seeing good policies being undermined.

The powerful victims are those women who lock into an ongoing victim status. They define themselves as victims and therefore cannot be held responsible for what they do. They use techniques to reinforce their self-image of powerlessness but they rarely feel empowered because they believe in their own passivity. They have a limited form of power, and often use it against other women. It can help them to retain a position of influence, and it works best when it is full of significant silences, emotional overlays, and virtuous martyrdom. However, it can be used in relatively small ways to ensure that territory is protected. It cannot be described as leadership because it is powerfully reactive and rarely pro-active. It blocks but generally does not initiate and is often not explicit in its function.

## CHAPTER 11

# Housekeeping,
# Conformity
# and its Effects

One important area of power is in the household. Over the past few years there has been considerable public debate on the issue of unpaid work carried out in the home. This covers both the pressures of tasks and the negotiations within households on how and by whom they are performed, and whether the time spent on them should be valued and recorded as a satellite account of our GDP. As an indication of the scale of this unpaid work figures[1] show that the time spent on food preparation in the home makes it the biggest industry in Australia.

Recent figures on the quantum of housework done in heterosexual partnered households indicates that the responsibility still rests primarily with women. The figures collected since 1974 have shown no increase in housework by males and only a limited increase in the hours they put into child care. The biggest shift in the amount of time spent in housework takes place when cohabitation occurs: the number of hours increases for women and decreases for men. This does not appear to be changing dramatically despite women's increased participation in the workforce, though women appear to be unilaterally decreasing what housework they do.[2]

These results appear to hold whether or not the women are

in paid work. They also suggest that the household remains the domain of women, albeit reluctantly in the case of some women. There is evidence from some studies[3] that arguments about housework are a major reason for dissension and possibly for marriage breakdowns. While this is not the focus of this book, it offers a micro site to illustrate some of the issues of gender and power.

Home disputes become tangled between issues of paid and unpaid work. Unpaid work is often not valued in the same way as paid. However, household work is a good means of servicing others, thereby creating obligations and generating guilt.

We can no longer claim positions of relative vulnerability derived from the almost constant, and often involuntary physical aspects of child bearing and rearing. Now that we can control our fertility and have access to paid work as well as unpaid, we cannot necessarily claim the right to concentrate on housework. So the expectation that the male must be the provider is becoming redundant. I recognise that in most cases, he can earn more, but this is slowly changing. The assumption that he will be prepared to support the woman and the children long past the stage when children need constant attention is not sustainable.

Of course, children should have time with their parents, but not just with one parent exclusively. Therefore, it is hard to justify public purse support for one adult to stay at home, except maybe in the child's first year. The basis for negotiation of the relative contributions in the home and in the workplace should be purely between partners.

This is often seen as an unequal relationship, within which

women are vulnerable to being bullied and forced into subservience. However, this may not be the only, or even dominant, model. There is the strong possibility that many women are claiming what they perceive as their 'right' to be supported in the traditional role.

Men have rarely had the option of being supported and their socialisation makes dependency on others very uncomfortable. Unemployed men and those out of the labour force often have severe identity crises. There are numerous studies which indicate that women who want paid work are also adversely affected by staying at home full-time.

Some women would maintain that they are partners with men and they provide the care of children, the housework and the community work, which in unpaid terms equates to men's provision of the funds. This may well have been the case once, but now hardly seems to hold. Of course, any couple has a right to arrange their relative contributions as they wish. But I would suggest that long periods out of paid work are quite disabling for both women and men.

The research I did with Helen Leonard on skills used in unpaid work[4] showed that even those who were always occupied at reasonably skilled unpaid work had serious difficulties in both recognising and valuing those skills. We also need to realise that there are women whose time spent in unpaid work is neither efficient nor productive if assessed in terms of time spent versus output on either physical or emotional levels. In other words, not all women who stay at home to look after kids and the household do a good job.

By accepting the primacy of the household responsibilities, the need to be the maker and mender of relationships and the main carer within the private sphere, women have a defined and valid role. The question is whether this is sufficient in itself to provide sustained interest and identity. A woman may also seek to have some outside interests: paid work, community activities including unpaid work, some social, cultural and recreational activities.

In a traditional household the woman is generally the second income earner; her role is not to make the base budget, even if what she earns is actually a significant contribution. Her 'choice' is to be at home for the children and for the husband. This situation varies in the mix of roles with many women 'having' to take on paid work when the money does not stretch. The model of essentially separate spheres, of man as provider and woman as housekeeper, defines the perceptions of both parties. Where the income is adequate, this model allows a woman to opt not to take on paid work, to choose to stay home with the children, to put her energies into assisting her husband with his career options.

Women in this category can sometimes be threatened by any suggestion that this role is not god-given, and therefore the best model of child rearing. By immersing themselves in this area full-time, they control the household work, often demanding gratitude but little input from other family members. They have defined the mother role as their power base and making it appear both time consuming and difficult is one way of attracting praise and power. In using their tasks to fill their day and by setting this up as a heavy load, these women establish a victim power model.

There are many questions to ask about this traditional gender division, particularly as technology and family size reduce the quantum of housework. Why do we have houses one third bigger now than postwar? And why do women spend similar amounts of time on housework now as twenty years ago? These questions raise serious issues of whether the role of full-time housewife/mother can, in itself, provide enough interest and stimulus for an adult male or female.

While writing this book I was reading about Hanna Arendt's philosophy and was taken with her belief that the optimum human condition is a mix of family and nurture, paid work and what she called active life.[5] Active life is cooperative action on behalf of others, doing something for others and self in the wider world. She saw the need for a balance between these three aspects. If any became dominant, then we become damaged societally and personally.

By being good and compliant, women have referred money and social standing, derived from their husbands' status. They may even have a sense of referred power, the power to influence a male in senior positions in his decision making. And they have an apparent history of gender relations against which to measure themselves: their mothers' generation, or that of their grand-mothers, books, films and soaps in which this model is still portrayed.

Home may be where the heart is, but for some women the heart bleeds with a sense of sacrifice. Home can provide a fertile breeding ground for victims, where we learn to play the support system and men learn how being active 'out there' lets them off most home-based activities.

Where once there were other adults in the house or over the fence, families today are smaller and more privatised with little local contact. There are so few adults in the home during the day that children become the only ones requiring emotional and physical care, and women who stay at home have power over the children.

Under these circumstances, women frequently express feelings of being overworked and overlooked, and make demands for public attention and recognition. Women with full-time home roles want these to be recognised as equal to workplace roles, ignoring the fact that most women with paid jobs do household work as well.

While there has always been debate on the relative merits of women's household contributions, their roles as social control agents are not so often canvassed. Women may not find intrinsic satisfaction in the repetitive tasks of housework and physical care. So it is easy to understand their animosity when they come up against a rhetoric which expounds the value of unpaid work and traditional roles while ignoring the reality of cyclical drudgery broken up by periods of nurturing.

The public policy debates on recognising women's unpaid work in the home and community offer a perspective on this. Survey results collected in 1992[6] showed that the most overworked mothers were those who combined full-time work and child rearing. They spent the longest time in paid and unpaid work and managed to spend two-thirds of the time on household and child care of those with no paid work. Recently some new time-use figures from the Australian Bureau of Statistics (ABS) also showed that comparative time burdens were on paid workers.[7]

Those with part-time employment spent 88 per cent as much time on household and child-care work as did those with no paid work, losing time that could be spent on sleep, leisure and education. In a write-us-a-postcard project run by the Australian Council of Women, processed by Distaff Associates, there was a strong write-in campaign from women who wanted tax splitting, wages for stay-at-home women and other forms of public subsidy. The anger and venom which framed the words on many of the cards was striking. The respondents painted themselves as being the only group contributing their unpaid labour, ignoring all evidence that their contributions in homes and community was not excessively more (one hour on average) than those with paid work.

Other projects, mainly focus groups run by state and Federal governments, gave further evidence of the attitudes of these women. Presumably, their spouses were often picked as 'good providers' who would validate the women's choice to stay at home. Women actively accepted this as their desired outcome. They were good wives and mothers and apparently comfortable with this as their ambition.

Their anger at not being appropriately validated by the wider community for their role is somewhat odd given that they have chosen to stay at home. Their animosity is genuine and painful, if misdirected. They blame feminists, including me, for attacking them and their position. I also meet women at meetings or through the media who feel this anger. They constantly accuse me, and other public feminists, of ignoring their contributions and putting them down.

As a public advocate for women to move from ascribed traditional roles, I often debate these critics on air. I try to offer some figures to prove they are neither the only ones doing housework and child care, nor are they the mainstays of voluntary community work. However this only seems to make them angrier. It took me a long time to work out why they were so hostile. Initially I, and most other feminists, apologised and bent over backwards to assure women at home that they were making a valuable contribution and one that should be recognised. I wondered why they saw public condemnation when there was so little in my view. In fact, the public debate and often the personal ones continue to validate the legitimacy of the choice to stay home. Apart from myself, women with paid work rarely mention women at home, except to acknowledge their contribution. The tentativeness of working women in discussing this area suggests that they feel some sense of guilt, even now, for not being at home.

Why are these women so angry? The most logical explanation comes from the voices of the women at home themselves. The two major complaints from stay-at-home women are about lack of money and lack of satisfaction. These they see as public issues, conveniently forgetting that many of them made the choice to stay at home. It is not surprising that many women are unsatisfied given that most of the tasks of housework are less than stimulating or enthralling.

This lack of satisfaction establishes internal conflict for some women at home. They are playing their womanly role; good women enjoy being at home. If they are bored, they therefore cannot be good women. This depression and low self-esteem turns into anger at the world for failing to make the housewife feel good even when she is being good.

Of course this is not the case for all women at home. Many enjoy time with their children, particularly with small babies and toddlers. When women take breaks at home as part of a defined life path, this is quite different. Some women without paid employment make careers in unpaid work and they may develop identity and self-esteem though committing considerable time and energy to this role. There are costs in this though, as women tend to undervalue their unpaid skills.

At this point it would be interesting to see the numbers of women in and out of the paid workforce. The ABS Labour Force Statistics for September 1994 record that 55 per cent of women between 15 and 69 years of age are employed; 6 per cent are unemployed; and 39 per cent are not in the labour force.

## Skills and expectations

Many of us never overcome our sense of guilt if we believe that we have failed in our duty as housekeepers. This is a realistic response to a social system which both expects women to be the household manager and to be at fault if they do not do it well.

Once when I was on air talking about housework to a male interviewer, he claimed his partner had no patience with his efforts and her standards were too high. The next day I met the woman at a conference and she was cross about his remarks. 'After all', she said, 'People judge me on the state of the house, not him, never mind who does the job'.

Any of us, me included, can relate to this; we panic at the thought that visitors will judge us, or mothers will always find something wrong. If you clean up before a cleaner comes so the house is not too dirty, or fail to use a cleaner because you would be embarrassed at the state of the place, you have a bad case of household guilts.

Amongst those skills women learn at home, and which are often undervalued or overlooked, we can include some less desirable skills in indirect manipulation. Playing the victim may once have been useful when there was a very large physical and economic imbalance in households and a swag of work to be done. Now these negative skills add to everyone's frustrations.

This was the bargain: the man worked and the woman kept house, and they used their different power bases to establish the relationship between them. However, this raises questions of whether those particular skills of indirect and victim power learned in the home are appropriate in the hopefully more egalitarian households which two incomes may bring, or useful to women in the workplace. Here men usually have greater authority which goes with their higher positions, with a more easily aroused aggression, and greater economic power. They may also have their training in sport, which has taught them effective use of competition and aggression as well as leadership and team work. Although they may use these too much and therefore misuse power, they have the basic transferable skills.

Women tend to fall back on techniques which they remember worked at home. They may use these on other women as well. The process of indirect control and the use of other techniques of discipline, such as withdrawal of love and approval, echo means by which some of us control children or the in- and out-group games we played with each other's emotions, while the boys played ball.

The household has been the one site in which women were recognised, albeit through their support roles. If we can look more closely at what men do and don't do in the home it may assist us in finding solutions to the quandaries raised in the women and leadership debate. If we can make the power roles at home less gender based, we might find a key to the major changes we need in our society.

### Onto the other foot

This material details an area in which a mixture of resistance and compliance created a form of power which may now have passed its use-by date. However, the way we react to our situation has possible consequences that affect our aspirations or obligations to leadership. What has centuries of being seen as the Other in the community done to women?

We continue to ask permission to talk and to be part of the wider process. Our speaking style is apologetic and tentative, and often easily silenced. Too many women feel they are not yet ready to be part of the process of change, that they have insufficient skills. This is why we sit waiting to be asked to take part in a process in which we feel we do not belong.

During my recent years as a consultant we did a lot of research into women and career planning. One of our major findings was that women waited far too long before they tried for more senior jobs or promotion. They perpetually felt that they were not ready; they did not know enough, they lacked experience. Yet they all reported that they saw men whom they considered less prepared, apply for the jobs and sometimes get them.

'Wait to be asked, don't be pushy ... if you are good your turn will come': these words are engraved in too many of our psyches for comfort. And we are still impressing this sentiment onto our daughters in less obvious ways. We still reinforce the cooperative, helpful aspects of girls and the competitive edge of boys. We still expect young women to be good girls and tend to overlook the more strident behaviour of boys as natural. It is this differentiation which reinforces feminine passivity.

We have all seen the phenomenon of confident, pre-adolescent girls growing fearful and tentative within a couple of years. Girls who were once leaders become followers and compliant, losing themselves in the process of growing up.

In their book *Mother-Daughter Revolution*,[8] Diebold, Malave and Wilson describe the process by which they feel mothers betray their daughters. They discuss how young women are silenced, and explain how mothers are often complicit in this.

They know what it means to grow up female and they want to help their daughters share the pleasures and avoid the pain.

Diebold et al identify some processes that occur in many households by which mothers, in seeking to protect their daughters, may actually put them at risk. The three authors combine their own experiences with professional skills and a wide input from new research into what happens to young women. They do not cast blame by writing of others' misdeeds, but share their experiences as women, mothers, activists and professional researchers to illustrate their case. They present a web of life experiences which many of us share, and use it to illustrate how young women are not encouraged to speak out. They report the way media and school reinforce the process of reducing girls' self-confidence by presenting them with body images and social prescriptions which reduce their sense of individual value. And they show how the manner in which women react can encourage either rebellion or compliance.

I am reassured by the way the authors trace this problem as an outcome of a complex set of processes which affect young women's sense of identity. They recognise that these are socially determined, not genetically programmed, or at least, that socialisation can counter the disputed effects of our genes and hormones. That means we can change it, and in particular, this change can start in every home.

The authors identify the ways in which we may unknowingly reinforce the messages of the dominant culture. Women may act as agents of compliance, not because we hate our daughters or want to harm them but because we want to protect them from the dangers of non-conforming. In doing so, we inadvertently put them at even greater risk by reducing their ability to find their own voice, let alone a public female voice.

Girls read more and are less prone to fight. They rebel in small ways but are less likely to do so in ways which attract the attention of teachers. They may excel more than boys in terms of overall marks at school and are seen as more accepting of the rules of the institution, and are better behaved. However, being well-behaved and receiving good marks do not seem to result in girls becoming successful leaders. The types of behaviour that are validated in boys, even though they get into trouble, are closer to those characteristics of aggression and risk taking which are likely to be rewarded in the wider society.

The way young women deal with growing up is by losing some of the sureness they had as pre-adolescents. They are socialised into forgoing the consequences of being seen as powerful. The rewards of the social system are clearly illustrated by the media, school and the world in which we move; men are the main arbiters of what should be and women can operate within these parameters and subvert but not challenge the ruling system.

This has led to male and female cultures arising that set parameters and standards for the behaviour of both. For women, the message is to attach yourself to others to gain power. Even 'mentoring', in the new language of corporate women, suggests that progress comes from attaching oneself. Moving out on your own is a no-no. The signal here is clear: those who move out too far are to be discouraged.

For men the lesson is different but probably no less

constraining: that you have to do it yourself. You need to know the rules and rites of passage and you can have a peer group and possible patrons. But it is up to you to make it, and there is no penalty for being seen to put yourself forward.

These very simplified versions of the stereotypes come back to the issue of power. Women experience men as powerful. It is our difficulty in establishing ourselves as subject, in control over any part of our lives, that sets us up to become passive resisters.

Maybe this section sounds a note of caution. We need to look at the conditions in which women are welcomed and see what the costs are. We must ask whether the institutions we are joining are doing a good job, or whether they need changing. We have to determine what we can alter that will bring about changes for other women too.

Too many women are complicit and compliant in a process which reduces our capacity to lead. This occurs at both senior levels and at the community level where women either duck leadership roles or undermine those who take them on. Such behaviour is not innate but comes from a feminine response to male power. We have learned these roles as powerless women and we reproduce and police them in institutions as a means of maintaining the status quo by defining both male and 'not male' standards.

It is not only men who block the way but our own inability to support the rebels and the leaders. It is women's discomfort as individuals with the women who buck the system that reduces our power to succeed. It is the way many women's groups operate which reduces the capacity of tall poppies to operate within these groups and also in the wider society.

# PART THREE

# About Men

This chapter contains some strong views and images which male readers may find uncomfortable. It is like the sealed section in *Cleo*; only for those who will not be offended.

This might sound like dramatic trivialising, but it is actually a serious attempt to look at the claims made by groups of men who feel that they have been discriminated against by the power of women. These groups have gained considerable public attention over the past couple of years and have managed to line up some female supporters as well.

I am not denying that men face problems. In fact, my arguments given in previous chapters are often built on concerns I have with the peculiar forms of masculinity our leaders and the media are promoting, and the effects these have on both men and women. I am committed to alternatives that I hope will free many men, as well as women, from inappropriate stereotypes of aggressive, individualistic masculinity.

Backlash movements are both wrong and unconstructive in their approach to male problems. I have had debates with Warren Farrell, author of *The Myth of Male Power*,[1] and some of his local followers, and I am very aware of the level of anger they feel towards women and their assumptions that women, and in particular feminists, are the problem.

As the previous section showed, I have no investment in portraying women as saints. Nor am I prepared to defend all the manifestations of feminism, and will happily acknowledge some irritations myself. However, I cannot find any logic in the particularly virulent attacks on mainstream feminism which assume that women have taken over and are now, for example, setting up health and education programs to disadvantage men. Nor have we taken over the Family Court, the Police Force or the criminal justice system in order to manufacture charges against men for domestic violence or sexual harassment.

While some male commentators are not taken seriously, others fan the often receptive flames of the media, and excite those who enjoy a good stoush. By setting up feminism and feminists as a dark and all-consuming force that targets men, advocates of a certain type give voice to all the other misogynist forces and create serious problems for women in general and feminists in particular.

Before we look at possible solutions, I want to outline some of the problems coming from men who would see themselves as protecting their sex against women. After that warning, you proceed at your own risk.

## The Demon Other

Sara Paretsky, in a visit to Sydney in 1994, drew parallels between the Protocols of Zion, an anti-semitic attack used to justify killing Jews, and anti-feminist rhetoric. She is a popular writer of feminist detective stories and was discussing the reactions of some of her fellow crime writers to her success. Her reference to the Protocols of Zion shows how seriously she took the levels of hostility she encountered. Her accounts mirrored some of what we have experienced here, though less overtly.

My targets in this chapter are those men who vent their anger and pain in public spheres, blaming women and various feminisms for their woes. They seek out women like me who are publicly visible and seem to re-create us, to ascribe to us all the ills they have suffered. The last year or so has signalled a new and more vocal set of defenders of men against women.

I acknowledge that a few men have legitimate gripes about being blamed by some women for the sins of other men. In political fights we tend to use slogans and there have been a few which generalise and simplify. Others get caught in the media's desire for the ten-second grab. Being polite and measured has rarely made news. Were the present advocates for the misery of men just balancing some angry women this would not be such a problem but this is not the case. The complainants are using positions of authority in universities or the media to allocate blame to all feminists. The media, of course, love such a debate.

I was recently contacted by a senior journalist who wanted to know why a man critical of feminism had been excluded from a conference at which I was speaking. Did this suggest an imbalance? As there were already many male speakers at the conference, I was puzzled as to why he felt excluded. Apparently, he had written letters to the organiser, copied for the media, claiming that my presence showed that the feminists were taking over, for which he garnered considerable media coverage.

I thought of the many battles I have had to wage to be included in a range of male dominated debates. Had I issued a letter of complaint if I had been excluded, the media would not have paid any attention. Of course, outspoken feminist troublemakers can be excluded from all sorts of forums with impunity, and always have been. However, the minute a man claims to be overlooked, in pain or discriminated against by women, he gets the sympathy vote and becomes the media's darling. Serious male researchers who carefully explore gender issues without wanting to blame women are not nearly as sexy.

It is the women-blaming lot that worry me as their efforts have enormous impact on the media. These are often angry, aggressive men whose writings and speeches set up the world as a conflict between men and women, with men as the losers. Women, to them, appear all powerful and representative of the mothers they hated, the wives who left them or potential sex partners who may reject them.

## Educating men

The education debate provides me with a recent example of how damaging male backlash can be. There have been programs for girls over the past decade which have helped to make the school environment more friendly for them and induced them to take on non-traditional subjects and careers. These programs attract small amounts of funding, and have created some positions within the education system and the inevitable conferences and task forces to plan, implement and monitor them. At the same time, retention rates for girls have risen and passed those of boys, some of whom leave school to take up apprenticeships or other courses. There are indicators that girls have surpassed boys in certain subjects and overall school results. In the same period, boys' retention rates have also increased and their performance has improved, though not as much as girls.

This is seen to prove that girls are doing better at the expense of boys. Therefore, the argument goes, the small resources going into girls' education should be redistributed to boys. This ignores the factors in the wider society that mediate girls' successes at school, the broader issues of school cultures and many other issues which could be used to refute the proposition that girls do better.

The presence of some limited additional resources for girls' programs has created a backlash of tidal-wave proportions. Piteous males are producing sheafs of statistics to prove that it is really boys who are having it tough. They are! And they always have been. The problems they face have not been exac-erbated by the changes for girls. It is a matter of inequalities, particularly for certain classes of boys, which put some of them behind the equivalent groups of girls. But it is not women who do it to them. It is the system set up by men for men which produces limited frameworks for masculinity and femininity. This fails to suit many boys as it was once shown to fail girls. With any signs of possible losses by boys to girls, the cries of indignation rival the summer cicadas, but are more strident.

The headlines are about poor boys, with no recognition of the many years when girls' non-performance was never even mentioned. Schools are mini reflections of a broader society still run by men.

The limits of girls' programs are becoming obvious in that fifteen years after retention rates evened, we still do not see an equivalent level of progress in post-school salaries and status for young women.

The amount of attention given to the problems of boys well outweighs the attention girls have received. The 1994 HSC (Higher School Certificate) results emerged in New South Wales to a chorus of media complaint that boys are losing out to girls. There are more girls than boys completing the HSC and this is considered an advantage for girls and ignores the fact that many boys have already transferred to trade courses in TAFE.

Girls comprise 48 per cent of those placed in the first thousand in the HSC, increasing from 35 per cent only six years ago. Far from being celebrated this is seen as a threat, and fears are expressed that in 1995 girls may exceed 50 per cent. So either we can start a process of slanging off with statistics, trying to prove that our constituency is more poorly serviced than the other in a fight for the few resources allocated to student equity issues, or we could look at the school culture and budgets and work together to make them more responsive to the needs of all students.

In the 1970s, women recognised that many of the problems in education affected both boys and girls. Many were involved in education reform and examined girls' education as part of an overall critique of the system. We knew that programs for girls were a stopgap solution; that real change would come when the culture and practices of the education process were changed. If boys are also victims, surely the time has come to fix the whole system!

This example provides a metaphor for the two ways of working. Feminists have often brought women into government services by setting up side programs to create equity because we have not had the power to influence the dominant masculinity. If we are to change the systems by which our society operates, we need access to mainstream funding, not just the equity units. If we have evidence that the mainstream system works for neither boys or girls, then let's work in tandem to bring about change.

Because women are still outsiders and have limited access to real power, our criticisms are often public and have to be forceful to get a run. This does not add up to 'a society which is very critical of men',[2] since most aspects of popular culture and other media, such as economics and sports pages, celebrate competition, violence and conformity to male Norms, not Norma!

### Defining the problem

There are many men who feel under-rewarded and under-appreciated and want to find someone to blame. Some do experience pain and anguish at having to carry the burdens of manhood. They feel quite correctly that their choices have also been limited by stereotypes. There are also some women who feel men are having it tough because women have changed the rules. They want to move the clock back, believing it was better for everyone then.

Terry Lane's 'Ode to the Common Man' in the *Good Weekend* magazine[3] set up a straw feminism, then knocked it down with selective quoting. His plaintive tale of the grey men who carried the world's woes and were blamed by women for them, offered feminists as the problem.

My response, also published in the *Good Weekend*, called 'A Bedtime Story for Terry Lane'[4] tried to answer his attack. Many women enjoyed my article, having skipped reading his, and I suspect most men did not read mine. If this is the pattern by which each side collects its advocates, we will continue to spend too much time in these futile pursuits. By setting up stereotypes, then knocking them down, commentators like Lane create prejudice rather than debate. Feminists are a broad church: the same range of views will be found in most large population groups. There are feminists who take simplistic views, and others, who, finding their carefully argued cases cut to a ten-second grab, are encouraged to extremes to gain headlines.

Shock horror stories about women's issues get frequent runs by journalists looking for the best conflict headline. Judges' comments, domestic violence orders, sexual harassment charges, lack of child-care places, homelessness, incest, rape and so on, are the 'women's issues' the media follow up.

The media bosses amply reward the upholders of both mainstream and extreme masculine views. They love male martyrdom and consistent anti-feminist sniping, but have a very short fuse for any similarly strong feminist views. Opportunities for an avowed feminist to have access to writing regular and extended opinion pieces in any form of media are rare.

To be commentators and columnists we must be seen as balanced and fair.

There are, of course, many feminists writing columns, doing regular commentaries and writing features. I know many closet media feminists who feel limited in their ability to express opinions, as their role is to be a journalist. However, they are a small minority and viewed as suspect if they do not show balance. On the other side, there are regular columnists and commentators who feel free to rail against feminists and feminism, political correctness and anything that takes their fancy without any need to maintain an appearance of balance. They are always ready to take up the cudgels of afflicted men and never look at the other side.

Why shouldn't we be angry if our views are not given the same access and are often derided and discounted? Sometimes these frustrations come out as intemperate judgments since many of us, me included, are left only with access to brief grabs or letters to the editors to argue our case against damage by these accepted commentators. I realise that there are angry men, misogynist men and others who have grudges against women individually and as a group. What worries me is that they seem to have a credibility that angry women have never achieved.

For two weeks in early 1994, ABC radio aired a program about men called 'Male Matters'. I was writing this book at the time and I was interested in some of the issues men raised. Most related to feelings, to relationships, to fathering and a range of concerns which are more generally seen as women's issues. Fine as far as it went; here were men asking for change, wanting to heal their pain and to share the responsibilities in the family which had been left to women. These were middle class, articulate men, making their case for relief from some of the tasks of manhood and demands of masculinity.

But where were the trade-offs? What were these men prepared to change about other aspects of their lives? Their focus was on individual choices and change. I recognised that these were personal statements and were not placed in a broader political context. Towards the end of the two weeks I expressed my concern to the executive producer of the program: 'What about shifting the gender balance in leadership? What about power?'

Their responses indicated to me that most men lobbying for changes only want them for their own benefit. The issues raised by the men were about creating more options for emotional and personal choice. The question of whether they were prepared to share the leadership load was not on their agenda. No mention of changes in power structures or institutional dominance by men was even considered. I cannot see the flowering of demands for male rights being anything more than a bid for attention at a personal level, not overall reform.

Many men in power love to have their prejudices reinforced. Maybe the men who do this fail to realise that they are undermining all debates on gender and sabotaging our attempts to change the system. I know some feminists who go spare when confronted with the 'new male victims' because they realise this undermines the concept of gender change.

## Male competing victims

I would like to warn those men who are competing with women for the sympathy vote—you should seriously consider whether it is worth the effort. There are few long-term gains in the process and the overall result may be a loss for both men and women. We need to amend both sets of inappropriate gender prescriptions as actors not victims.

*Victim:* my thesaurus gives options including 'dupe' and 'fool' as well as 'prey' and 'dead'. None of these are very attractive options, yet for over a decade we have seen the phenomenon of purported victims competing for public attention and funding.

Warren Farrell sells his book by complaining about the way women have abused men. Like the 1950s recanting Reds of the 'I was a communist for the FBI!' model, Farrell is a recanting 'feminist' who sets up a mix of factual and specious evidence for the victimisation of man. When I was to appear on television with him, I was tempted to go through the pages of his book, finding counter evidence, his statistics against mine—a duel of means and medians. Had I done this, I would have portrayed myself as a publicly feral feminist in the ultimate contest between the sexes for the most powerless prize. I could probably win some arguments, but in the process I would also lose. Playing competing victims is a dangerous game.

Moves to market forces mean increased competition between disadvantaged groups for the ever-diminishing public dollars. This is one area where competition is neither efficient nor effective as it sets powerless groups in conflict. This often means the spoils go to the best public sympathy evoker, not the most legitimate. When competing victims hit the gender issue, the possible outcomes are likely to be grim for all 'victims', male and female.

One of the problems is that creating victims means defining villains. When women created themselves as victims, men were cast in the role of villain. They fitted the bill: they fill gaols, are convicted of most assaults, perform most murders, and so on. Of course, not all men are villains but their over-representation in the formal areas of perpetrators makes them an easy target. Whether it was justified or not, the existence of a group that can be identified as the enemy is a shorthand way of attracting public attention. If you want attention for the plight of victims of sexual abuse or domestic violence, you do better with a defined villain. Otherwise, if it is seen as the victim's fault, there is no real priority placed on limited public resources.

Men were a convenient hook on which to hang a critique of the reason for all the violence in society. Their problem behaviours are often unacceptable extensions of what was once defined as acceptable masculine behaviour. Their images of masculinity in sport and popular culture, in war and even in high culture, valorise strength and winning, and make no clear lines between good and bad. These standards are set by men who still hold most of the formal power. There is a powerful woman here and there, but the senior ranks are still overwhelmingly male. So, for feminists, defining men as the problem seemed logical if maybe somewhat simplistic. It was the masculinity of particular powerful, elite men that they targetted.

In the victim modality of the men's movement there is a failure to question the structure of our society, and an oversimplification of the problem as being that 'girls have gone too far, so it's time to move the boys forward'. Fundamental questions of masculinity and its privileges and power are not addressed. This is combined with the mythopoeic/Jungian (Iron Man) archetypal, therapy-based version of interpersonal grief and loss. Here victim envy raises its head in the form of ruling class males entering the stakes for pity-based attention and resources.

This competing victim syndrome has been part of public debate for some time now. The relative conservatism of the last decade has led to reductions in government spending and more competition for the compassion dollar. This has caused an inelegant scramble amongst those generally labelled special interest or social justice groups. These marginal groups usually represent those who have little or no access to those who make decisions.

The final absurdity is that white, anglophone, heterosexual, able males want to join the victims. They want their share of the marginal cake crumbs, ignoring the fact that they are demographically the group that actually makes the decisions about who gets what.

I find it confusing that our relatively small steps are seen by some men and women as a massive victory. Similarly, I find the current apparent level of fear and loathing of feminism hard to understand. We are neither super witches, responsible for the downfall of western civilisation as we knew it, nor currently threatening it. Would that we did have the power they see in us! Articles now abound which name feminisms and feminists as the cause of men's problems. I acknowledge that men have problems but I cannot understand how feminists are to blame for them.

Rather than blame us, men who feel they are having a rough time should be pleased that women have changed the agenda. Take health issues for a start. We have just managed to induce a shift in the priorities of the health-care system from production of major technological diagnostic toys to the introduction of widespread early screening tests which will hopefully prevent the need for major intervention.

This would seem to be a victory for commonsense but the responses are somewhat bizarre. Instead of men using this precedent as a model for, say, prostate cancer prevention, they attack the increases in funding of breast cancer research. Concerned men could pursue the same paths women have opened up, and see if still more money can be spent on health maintenance and screening. I would hazard a guess that they might manage that more easily than women did, as they are talking to other men about that very important 'part' they all seem anxious about. Or is it too hard to talk about, even amongst men? I am puzzled why these kinds of issues have been neglected, given their prime masculine importance. It says something about the way men deal with illness and their bodies that they have to wait till women raise the issue. This does not explain why they get angry with us, rather than targeting the decision makers.

## Toxic masculinity

If given a choice, would you trust your country to a member of a group that exhibits suicidal risk taking with poor self-care skills? Considering that he is also more likely to be gaoled, involved as perpetrator or victim of violence and die younger, is he worth grooming as leader? Would you consider that acceptable, appropriate behaviour involves high levels of aggression and competitiveness, together with short-term attention spans, and a lower than adequate grasp of the care necessary for exigencies of daily life?

This was my first response to the data on poor males produced by Richard Fletcher from the University of Newcastle.[5] He has collected pages of statistics indicating the disadvantages of men vis à vis women. These are intended to raise questions of the relative resources spent on men versus women but raise for me the question of the suitability of men to predominate in positions of power.

It is interesting that causal connections are not made between the statistical basis of men's earlier demise and the prescribed masculine mores with which they are asked to comply. It is not femininity that establishes the need for young men to achieve through physical risk taking. It is not feminine values that encourage the forms of male bonding that result in too much drinking and violence.

How useful are those characteristics that are deemed to be appropriately masculine? What functions are performed by the excess testosterone and adrenalin which men may claim as a source of their behaviour? Competitiveness, standing up for yourself, sticking up for your mates, proving physical prowess, winning etc, may be products of the socialisation of young males into the tribe or herd. The texts of sociobiology are full of examples of why we have had to breed for the survival genes.

What use have we for them now? Civilisation has made many of what have been called the 'animal' characteristics of man increasingly redundant. As humans we have developed social structures and laws to produce social behaviours and reduce the need for force as the determinant of power. Without wanting to promote a biological view, it is possible that we need to question whether the social/biological processes which give us certain masculine models of leadership are still appropriate.

In fact, all the clichés which assume that man is a testosterone driven animal do not hold: boys will be boys, or men are naturally aggressive, sexually on the prowl, competitive, self-interested, will fight for family, etc. There are boys and men who read novels and write about emotions, who are poets and dancers, and who establish their bona fides without having to engage in risk-taking behaviour. They, and others who eschew the typical at-risk behaviour of masculinity, need the acceptance of other men to validate their choices. If boys are scared of being labelled as unmasculine if they are seen to do well at school, it is other boys who set the standards, and the girls who reinforce them. If boys feel the cost of good school behaviour is to be an outsider in the male ethos, then it is from within male society that change must come.

This is, however, likely to be resisted. Expressed more academically by Bob Connell, 'masculinity exists impersonally as a subject position in the process of representation, in the structures of language and other symbol systems'.[6] He recognises multiple masculinities co-exist, for example, black and gay, but are subordinated, marginalised or complicit in the hegemonic process.

This is, as he explains, neither simple nor unitary. No man necessarily expresses his mode consistently but there is a consciousness of a 'patriarchal (masculinity) dividend' which is not to be lightly discarded. This can comprise material rewards in mixtures of income, access to power in organisations, honour and prestige and certain rights of service and passage.

## Women displaced

The evidence still shows that when men move into defined areas of female dominance, they move in at a senior level or rise very quickly. They are a novelty and the response is to nurture them and make sure they are appreciated. In fields like social work and librarianship, men have risen quickly through what were once very feminised occupations.

I remember in the 1970s, the first two men graduating with preschool qualifications moved straight into directors' positions. The desegregation of principals' job in the New South Wales education system at this time meant that men took almost all the available positions: as principals of girls' schools as well as many of the other senior jobs. These are only two of the many examples of male successes in what were previously female areas. And the trend continues today.

The reverse does not hold however. Women in perceived 'men's jobs' receive little or no advantage. Instead, they often find themselves regarded as interlopers and have to establish their bona fides by carefully working within the framework allowed. While there may occasionally be a woman who has benefited by being the first, the common pattern is for women to stay on the lower levels in male areas for at least as long, if not longer, than men.

The Doherty Report[7] on boys in the New South Wales education system bewailed the fact that few men were entering primary teaching and therefore were not available as role models for younger children. This was seen as exacerbating the problems of boys and so required urgent action. However, the lack of strong role models in the senior ranks for girls was not given nearly the same emphasis or prominence.

These major gender-based differences can be summed up by the proposition that those areas attributed to and dominated by males are considered to have relatively high prestige. Areas identified with women's attributes and numbers are seen as having less prestige. It is pertinent, however, that the gender balance has more to do with the prestige of areas than the inherent value of the work itself.

## Double deficits, doubly deficient

Most of the 1970s debates on gender issues in education worked on a deficit theory. This assumed that there was a norm and the norm was male. Therefore, the goals established were assumed to be necessary to achieve gender parity. These involved increasing retention rates, greater participation by girls in those fields of education dominated by boys and improving results for girls in those subjects where boy's marks were generally significantly higher. Even then, boys were failing in the areas where girls did well. However, with the exception of literacy, this was not seen as a problem. It was assumed that the consequence of this would be women moving into traditionally male working areas, thus reducing inequities in jobs and wages, for example. Now, a couple of decades later, we have an interesting change with men using a mixture of health and education figures to demand equity with women.

I notice that the double deficit theories about men are limited to those few areas in which women dominate and which men avoided because they were seen as powerless, such as the humanities and interpersonal skills. These men have not indicated a desire to move in big numbers into household domestic arts so they can practise their bedmaking skills for the increasing number of jobs in hospitality and community service areas. The fact that many of these paid work opportunities require skills learned in the household has been partly why they have always been undervalued as paid jobs.

Where are the deals and trade-offs in the men's claims for more access to female realms? There is no evidence that men are shouldering any significant responsibility for housework[8] despite the desires of over 90 per cent of women that they increased their share of housework.[9] The Doherty Report supports the proposals for more men in junior school jobs, and more women in senior positions.

Where are the male supporters of feminist aims, acting as scouts to promote gender equity in major institutions? Surely this would be a logical step to ensure that the problems currently imposed by certain rampant masculinity-based value systems could be reviewed and humanised?

## Making changes

What I am largely wrestling with is the possibility for change in large organisations, including political, economic and community ones. There the forms of masculinity are institutionalised, so Norm continues to be clearly male. The practices of masculinity are not just part of the ruling elite but are built into the cultures of organisations.

We could start by insisting on boys taking on many of the areas in which girls excel. This might involve programs to reduce aggressive behaviour, less contact sports, more poetry, literature written by women, and behaviour modification designed to help boys pay attention.

What would the boys' advocates say if boys were domesticated, made to do housework for homework? Washing up may fit them for the emerging jobs in hospitality. Then they can join their sisters in jobs as kitchen hands and nurses' assistants. Some boys can share both girls' academic successes and their subsequent post-school failures to achieve money, power and influence.

Those pushing for the feminising of boys' educational outcomes have my support. I am interested in reducing the advantages that masculinity appears to bring, particularly as they may be anti-social as well. But those promoting change need to understand that this may undermine boys in the present job market. There is evidence that the choices girls make and their areas of dominance do not return material success.

## The cost of being a victim

Women have missed the point when we just measure ourselves against men. We need new standards but they don't need to include becoming surrogate men, or establishing an essential femininity as a revolt against the presumed characteristics of masculinity. Men also need to look at what they want, not just pick out odd bits of womanhood to incorporate into their personas.

Amongst others, I have been advocating for some time against the women's movement playing the victim game. This is hard because it is the role we have been allocated and it is the safest one for women to pursue. When feminists talk about rape, incest, domestic violence and the other aspects of gender power imbalances, they are working within a framework of women's issues. They achieve a series of small gains in the legal areas, sometimes by claiming special privilege, because they have found this to be successful. So we have achieved changes to the law on provocation and the laws on domestic violence.

There are aspects of the women's movement that have pushed the victim button very hard and long. It has been partly imposed by the general direction of public policy which demands pathos as a preliminary to shifting resources. A decade ago, I wrote a piece which said we had been allowed to pursue the victim issues because these were areas which were seen as women's issues, and they did not compete with the issues men saw as important. This still holds today.[10]

I can speak from my own experience, and those of many others, about the consequences of moving out from the accepted areas of discourse. Try being a feminist commentator on economics or foreign affairs; it is difficult to get a go! In the past thirty years, public debates have still sorted topics into those which are male (serious, rational and universal) and those that are female (sectional, emotive and sexual). I am a long way, therefore, from taking men seriously when they start on the competing victim syndrome. It reminds me of the times at conferences when I talk of changing power relationships in the wider society and some man stands up to tell me he often washes up!

There is no point in contesting the victim-of-the-moment role. We see the evidence of this as charities for local and overseas aid compete for donations with pictures of ever more pathetic or emaciated waifs. They are seeking to create an impulse to give by using pity but often create distance instead. Sympathy is a limited resource, empathy even harder to achieve, and one of the consequences of victim status is that we often drive away those we want to attract. People erect barriers between themselves and the objects of pity with which they do not wish to be associated.

## Changing the system

Our images of leadership seem limited to macho stereotypes. If this is so, what advantages could girls extend to boys at school? Maybe the real problem is in the qualities that our society rewards and the outcomes these produce. Maybe if these change, then both feminine and masculine characteristics will lead to success. While images of masculinity include dominance, and this equates with authority, men will be left to take on responsibilities for others. Concomitant with that appear to be the problems of their early death rates, crime rates, and other social and physical problems.

Balance these statistics against men earning more money than women, holding most of the positions of power and dominating most of the disciplines of learning. Maybe there is a connection and the burdens of power are causally linked to some of the downside damage.

So, if running the country and all its major institutions, managing the money in the major banks and companies, and doing two thirds of the paid work has its costs, is the solution a transfer across genders? Maybe with more time and space and genuine discussion, we could relieve men of the burdens of some duty and power. Maybe men could move away from the metaphors of battle and we could find ways in which we could all change the rules so they too would have more choices and fewer ascribed roles. But in the near future could those who want to indulge in trench warfare move into another paddock and find other little boys who want to play wargames.

Feminist Executive Toy

## CHAPTER 13

# Writing Futures

While writing this book, I have clarified my own thoughts about what women are doing, and what we could be doing. I have also become increasingly aware of the differences between joining the system and trying to reform it.

This section targets a range of outcomes, all of which are based on individual action. It is inevitably directed at you the reader, to those you may wish to talk to, and perhaps to organisations that may want to follow up some of the suggestions given here. I have combined ideas, which may lead you to different ways of seeing and defining problems, with some practical suggestions for possible actions. This section is designed to help you feel more confident to lead, more comfortable with the concept of power, and more likely to support other women who take risks.

## Present participating

This is the active part of the process which will involve you in deciding what you feel comfortable doing, and then moving outside the comfort zones as we come to realise that change is never comfortable for long.

As I wrote the headings for this book it struck me how often

I was using the present participle, the one where verbs are turned into nouns by adding '-ing'. This is the present continuous participle, which can be used as noun or verb. I hope this old grammatical term can provide us with a metaphor for on-going action.

## Making (o)u(r)topias

Utopia—the perfect future we often cannot imagine—is sometimes part of religious beliefs or political theories. Making one (or more) that fits feminist principles is going to be hard. There are plenty of generalisations about utopian futures where everything miraculously turns out to be civilised and pleasant. However, the steps by which we move from our present situation towards what we want are rarely articulated. So we tend, like other discontented groups, to work within what is and not clarify exactly where we want to be.

For the last few years I have become increasingly conscious of the lack of options available to us; of the apparent inability of groups, critical of the status quo, to do more than criticise. One of the major faults of many movements has been the lack of explicit plans and goals for progress.

What would you do if you were prime minister for the day? Realistically, you would probably spend the time arguing with your mostly male Cabinet, or doing battle with your mostly male senior public servants. But if you could have three political wishes, what would they be?

Write them down. If you find the task too hard, start with three little wishes, just some tidying up of the present system.

Then practise going more global till you get into the swing of having political fantasies.

If you started with some really big wishes, such as abolishing war or saving forests, move down the scale a bit now. Sometimes too big is also too distant and we become overwhelmed by the problem, let alone trying to come up with solutions.

Part of the process of change is to decide what is possible and what issues we feel are worth doing something about. This can begin with the familiar—many powerful women I know started at the local level. One was cross about a council's refusal of her plans for a new bathroom and went on to become mayor of a large council. Others worked on school crossings, saved historic buildings, set up playgroups, counselled breastfeeding mothers and ran local election campaigns or similar activities. Some then dropped out, some stayed local, others moved into wider spheres.

My history, for example, is not atypical: I joined a new organisation called the Women's Electoral Lobby (WEL) in 1972. It was focused on an upcoming Federal election, the one which ousted the Coalition government after 23 years. I had had some previous involvement in supporting peace issues and a spurt of political activism at university, but on fairly limited levels. Suddenly I was in the limelight as women were very much on the political agenda in the election that year. I found my voice and vocation and have been involved and public ever since. I realised at an early stage of public life that I was articulate and argumentative, but more importantly, I also noted that most of the men in the public eye were neither more expert, nor brighter than I was. So there seemed no reason for my silence or deferral to them.

WEL waded in where angels were supposed to fear to tread. We tackled politicians and the media, admittedly in an environment where the women's movement was a novelty. We were lucky in that sense, but we also made our own luck. We worked hard to sound credible. We read and asked questions and rapidly became informed. We also took risks, butting into areas where there was little information and few sources on the inside that could help us find out what was going on. Sometimes we succeeded and other times we had to try again.

We also built trust and support in the group, and this process worked for quite a few years. The experiences I had and the friendships made in those early years fuel my belief that there are women who can create working feminist cultures which can provide politics and pleasure, and effective action. I am optimistic about what is possible and how, hopefully, having more women in leadership roles can achieve positive changes.

### Changing the leadership

In previous chapters I looked at some of the criticisms of current leadership that are being raised in the context of senior managers and management generally. There are however, few definitive books on what constitutes good, alternative leadership, and it may well be an impossible task to define this. Obviously the leadership skills necessary to guide people up a mountain or fight a bushfire may be very different to those we need for daily tasks or routine politics.

We need to recast some of the debates about leadership and question when and why we need certain types of leadership, rather than assume a universal set of skills. I have worked in organisations which have been 'over led'. In a big government department for example, where senior management worked in a constant state of crisis, with the consequence that structural changes were never made because crises always took over. Almost a decade later, this department is still trying to deal with the same problems because a culture of constant crisis and structural reviews continues to put their programs at risk.

There are other models of management, including what some text books identify as 'country club' management where the attention is on comfort rather than on progressing. Others run on command models with a very hierarchical system based on military lines. There are many types, and some will be valid for particular situations while others may be more broadly functional.

## Characteristics of leadership

The image of testosterone-driven, macho leadership is often a barrier for women, but this does not mean that all women would agree on what might be deemed to be feminine characteristics in leaders. While writing this book, I was also teaching research methods at the University of Technology, Sydney. I am indebted to some of my students for their permission to use the results of two projects.

While these were small training exercises, they explored areas not covered elsewhere. One asked approximately 200 men and women, evenly divided, about their concepts of leadership and gender differences. Another explored workplace issues with over 100 women, asking their views of women and men as bosses. The sample size in both was small and the sampling processes were not representative of the overall population; however the numbers were sufficient to use as interesting indicators.

A coincidence of the findings was that both surveys showed about two out of three respondents believed there were differences between women and men as leaders or bosses. As there were over 300 respondents, about one third male and covering diverse areas and occupations, the consistency of these findings is interesting. Also, there were no differences between the beliefs of men and women overall.

There were some indications that those in paid work were more likely to see differences between men and women bosses. Where differences were nominated, the workplace issues survey showed that women were more likely than men to be nominated as having both positive and negative differences. The respondents commented that one female bad-boss experience tended to be transferred to the whole category, while this did not occur in relation to male bosses.

When asked what characteristics were desired in leaders, respondents in the leadership project wanted strength (decisive, initiating, brave) as the first category, followed by ability to participate (team worker, listener, negotiator, approachable), then equally, to be caring (thoughtful, compassionate, tolerant, patient) and ethics (honest, trustworthy, respected, good example).

The surveys involved only small numbers but the findings are suggestive as all but the first category deal with people skills and therefore show a clear preference for leaders who can manage. Interestingly, a gender breakdown, interpreted with caution given the numbers, shows that women, more so than men, tended to support strength coupled with caring. Men went for participation and honesty as their top two preferences.

These results need further exploration but open up useful debates in terms of the proposition that we need a variety of leadership styles. While some of these styles will be task based or organisation based, others should also reflect the particular needs of the workers.

The wide perception of differences between male and female leadership styles adds impetus to the need for the introduction of more women so diversity can be legitimated for both men and women in leadership roles. Maintaining the diversity depends on changing the cultures of organisations so they do not eliminate new modes because they are alien and threatening.

## Making a new leadership environment

Without setting criteria for a female leadership model, let alone a feminist one, it is possible to set an agenda for more leading women. It would include:

- A whole life agenda—the integration of the public and private in both business and government so that decision making can include more perspectives and eliminate blind spots.
- A senior level movement to encourage integration of the demands of home, paid work and community so that everyone, women and men, can organise their lives into more balanced mixtures of work, community, family and leisure activities.
- A model to encourage broader choices of roles and responsibilities so that they are not primarily determined by gender; a

less gender deterministic division of labour in both public and private spheres. Therefore better management personally and organisationally of our human resources;

- Legitimising the entry of newly labelled and recognised skills, particularly those developed in the process of child rearing and housekeeping responsibilities, in decision-making arenas;
- Outsourcing and reorganising household chores so no one is expected to do more than their reasonable share;
- Offering alternative styles of leadership as appropriate options.

Implementing these suggestions is not going to be easy. Despite the rhetoric, evidence shows that workplaces are still not family friendly. To exemplify this I want to draw on some research Distaff did on telephone use in the workplace.[1] We had followed up some other work on the importance of telephones for those at home as a break from isolation, with research into the way telephones allowed people to manage the dual demands of paid work and family.

The research methodology was constantly amended because we ran into strong resistance from employers as to what exactly was perceived as the use of phones for personal calls in the work-place. Here was *chat* writ large—'just women gossiping' was the first reaction, and 'family needs are inappropriate in the work-place'. Even when we showed a cost benefit which affirmed the merits of explicit permission to use phones for family friendly workplaces, the resistance continued. Workplaces did not really mix with the outside world; management considered that the concerns of home and work should be kept separate.

At the end of the project, we mailed out 500 invitations to seminars we intended to hold. We had to cancel one and use personal contacts to fill the other. The general attitude when we rang around was that people preferred not to talk about the issue. The human resources/EEO staff we contacted knew that employees used the telephone at work to manage the home but were terrified that an acknowledgment of it would lead to clamp-downs. They felt any discussion of workplace links with home was still too dicey to raise in the mid 1990s.

This suggests that we need to do some work on the issue of work and the family as a high priority. Working hours of men in Australia are going up, not down. These show up in statistics and anecdotes where a culture of longer working hours is part of being seen to be efficient. In the film *The Firm* much is made of the billing hours of the young lawyers and this is illustrative of the often undue pressures that are put on those seeking to succeed, whether male or female.

This is totally antithetical to the effective combination of out-of-work parenting roles and senior work roles. It could be read as a barrier erected by those in the power streams to avoid being roped into care and to prevent women from entering that terri-tory. The gender divides are now topped with the cracked edges of the hourglass as time becomes a major barrier for those who also want time with families.

## Working at and from home

A change in work practices that should be monitored is telecom-muting. At first glance, this suggests a better means to combine work and care; by working from home, parents (read mothers) can be child carers and workers at the same time. This has many traps, however. Doing both jobs simultaneously is likely to be stressful: outworkers end up working late at night to get up any speed. Similarly, trying to make sense of work and deal with a fretful child is not an easy task.

Another more serious trap is that the other aspects of work we need, at least as much as money and interest in the job, are excluded. There is no sense of being with peers, no workplace community, no validation of self through contact with other adults who see you as a person, not an attachment to family members. Working from home could end up a very poor option unless clear working conditions are built in which include contact in person with others, access to communal facilities and resources, and time out of the home on a regular basis.

Interestingly, in what is being heralded as the post-industrial era, there are signs that the divide between paid work and home might slowly close. Men may also move back home to work and therefore, in theory, the home may be raised in status to a production unit again. However, this arrangement would still ignore the needs of say children or the housebound to find the company of others and outside activities that home-based care cannot offer.

### Leading on

Melding of the place of home and work together and changing the dysfunctional parts of both would allow more options for women seeking involvement in leadership. This framework also raises possibilities for a new structure for our society which is not based on the more masculine assumptions about the individual, but instead blends together the linked societies we are all part of while still acknowledging the needs of individuals.

This is a different and much more comfortable model for me and, I suspect, many other women, and preferrable to being self-contained and selfish. The leftover 1980s individualism about how to fix your psyche and develop your individuality still survives in management material, with the outcome that you are dependent on no one. While it has been a financial bonanza for those who sell courses on how to 'make it', this model lacks a social or ethical base.

Human beings are interdependent. We start that way and retain our need of one another to maintain a balance. Like a set of threads woven into a pattern, we are part of a social fabric in which our threads and strands tie us in place. These are the ties often identified with family and community, as the non-working part of our lives. Again perceptions about gender obscure the need for personal connections both in work and at home.

However, we are not simply members of the pack. We carry a responsibility for what we do to ourselves and others. Therefore we also need a sense of some separability, a sense of self and others, to find some boundaries within ourselves. Without this we would not be able to make our own decisions, to act independently and ethically, or to create change.

There will always be a constant tension for us between affirming our links and maintaining our sense of self. When we move too far towards the links we lose ourselves in the mob.

Pressures of conformity, for stasis and rejection of others give us cults, fundamentalism, nationalism, racism and other demands for the complete subjugation of the self. Individualism rampant gives us greed, amorality and chaos.

The line between can be hard to walk because we need all sides of self in order to be fully responsible adults. In recognising some of the aspects of the different views of self, we can develop alternate views on leadership. The concept of good leadership was (and is still) male, tough and rational; aggression was fine, sympathy suspect. Men also had to fit certain stereotypes, otherwise their chances of progress were inhibited too.

The linked system suggests that we need to develop leadership from within and not necessarily from the top: ways of developing shared responsibilities and using the mixes of skills of different people and ideas. Learning to work with each other, to create groups in which we can create relationships that are functional for completing tasks and running programs, presents us with a challenge that we must now meet.

## CHAPTER 14

# Taking Over

It is time we took responsibility not only for leadership but also for changing its current form. We need to offer alternate models for government and public services, and even for commerce and business to those currently in vogue. So how do we re-create the world? A fairly immodest question considering we would never all agree on the model we want to follow. However, one of my moments of great encouragement came from reading Charles Lindblom,[1] an American management theorist who wrote about 'muddling through'. In two articles written in 1959 and 1969 he explained his concept of social change.

Lindblom starts from the proposition that the world is too complex for grand theories of change to work. He offers as an alternative to what he calls 'root' change, 'branch' change. This is smaller, is easier to predict and manage and if you make a mistake, it is not drastic; but if you get it right you can move on to the next change. We can set medium term goals—what we want to do by the year 2000 in health, for instance. Then we can take a few small steps towards this goal and see how we go before taking the next one. In this way any mistakes we make will be small and probably reversible.

This is the politics of small reforms rather than the total

changes exhorted by Marx or markets. Both are grand theories that try to explain everything and have made some very big errors. We could argue that they were fatally flawed at the outset because of their masculine focus, and their failure to take into account the many areas of life that are the province of women.

We must extend the agendas of public debates to include what is now seen as private. This will allow us to integrate into policy making all the aspects of daily life that need attention, and avoid the mistakes made by ignoring them. This should also change the order of what is regarded as important, putting community and relationships up there with the economy.

I have my own ideas of what I would like to see in integrated, incremental plans for making the world, locally and globally, a better place. In Part One, I suggested we could move away from the focus on the individual to focusing on the way we are all connected. There are alternatives and we should begin to consider them because revolutions and change start when people believe they are possible.

No one is sure where the ideas for the future and the energy to carry them out will come from. I hope that women will contribute more. For a long time we have been ready to tell the world and its leaders what we think has been done badly or not at all; now we need to come up with new ideas and be prepared to put ourselves on the line and implement them.

### Surfing the adrenalin highs

This is often regarded as a frightening prospect for women. The images of power are not only masculine but often seem fairly joyless. This is not necessarily so—there are pleasures to look forward to. Power can provide a real high, a sense of almost orgasmic joy, a feeling of strength, effectiveness and control which can be quite intoxicating. This is one of the reasons why people hold onto it so tightly.

The desire for power can make people behave badly and stupidly, and often cause destruction. Having power can also lead to abuse by those individuals and groups in control. It was Lord Acton who said power corrupts, but absolute power corrupts absolutely. Translating this to a gender debate, it suggests there is substantial danger in leaving power so much in the hands of a relatively elite group of men. Having worked for those with power, and occasionally had small and sometimes not so small inputs into making changes, I have experienced power and felt its thrill. It can corrupt and distort because the highs become addictive.

## A different leadership—shared power

While I was writing this book there were two examples of what should become common occurrences. The major and public one was the celebration of the oldest femocrat office in the world, the Office for the Status of Women (OSW). The first public service advice unit to a country's leader set up by feminist lobbying had its twentieth birthday in November 1994. A book recording its history was publicly funded,[2] as was a big reception. The media loved it and *The Australian* ran sections of the book with a group photograph of the first aspirants to the position of women's adviser to the prime minister, including myself twenty years ago. Another newspaper ran an article raising the recurring question of whether we still needed an Office of the Status of Women.

The conclusion was yes, because the upper echelons of decision making are still mainly male. This need was reflected at the reception in the speeches given by the Prime Minister, Paul Keating, and his Minister Assisting on the Status of Women, Carmen Lawrence. They promised more women in Parliament once the imminent Labor Party Conference endorsed a quota of 35 per cent of women candidates in winnable seats by 2002.

The other event was a much smaller celebration, and a farewell. It was an exhibition of women's art and writing which took place in the warehouse from which I had operated as a consultant. Organised by Jan Wood, the eighty pieces on display were designed to show woman's strength.

It was the last major function at the office: a space that had nurtured a range of feminist activities over the past nearly five years with too little money and too few, often voluntary, resources. We could have continued in this endeavour if there were others to share the load and take responsibility.

We had no public funding so, unlike the government body, the time and resources for the exhibition were donated. It illustrated very clearly the difference between working from the inside as did the Office of the Status of Women, and working from the outside through the fragile collection of some ten groups which regularly used the space and its resources.

In the two days celebrating the twenty-year anniversary of

the OSW I ran a workshop on power and leadership for the staff of OSW, joined the elite invited to the reception, and was one of the opening speakers at the art show. I discussed some of the problems of women and leadership both formally and informally at these two events.

The formal structures of the bureaucracy and the lavish resources available for the OSW celebration contrasted with the minimal finances and simple organisation of the art show. Yet in both there were personal commitments and energy derived from the sense of gender injustices that fuels feminisms.

The processes raised many questions and offered some answers. The organiser of the art exhibition defied every precept in books of management. Without formal planning or money, Jan Wood used her vision to lead an extraordinary number of people to provide time, resources and energy for the project. This is not just a static exhibition but has already toured many country towns in a suitcase, picking up more exhibits on the way. After this, its destination was the United Nations' Women's Conference in Beijing.

This is leadership, not that Jan Wood would agree with me. She shares the plaudits with the women and family members who made it happen with her. An extraordinary confluence of energy brought it about but only because, with no formal support, she started the process and kept it going even as money ran out. This was a cooperative enterprise at all levels, lacking even informal hierarchies. It was not a collective because decisions were not taken to meetings but made on the run. There were no rules and processes decided on, just the job done. Jan Wood does not fit the image of the charismatic leader whose personal magnetism makes people do her bidding; her style is apologetic, enthusiastic and shows faith in people's goodness. This worked because people wanted to help make her vision possible. It was a pleasure to contribute because her leadership encouraged positive enthusiasm, and was not built on inducing guilt.

This example raises a much wider issue: how we recognise leadership. When I used the term at both events, the reactions were similar to those reported in the Introduction. The women saw male and physical or military images of leadership and these were not ones to which they could relate. The resistance to owning the concept of leadership was palpable.

However, there were ideas of where we could go in search of alternative models. A comment from an old friend raised the concept of supported leadership, a term that comes from counselling. This started a train of thought: leaders are so often seen as being alone and separated from the rest. This is, in part, a response to the ideas that commonly define positions of leadership: the buck stops here, the burdens of office, the power of one, the need to remember you are the boss. Formal organisations make it clear that power at the top must be just that and reject the possibilities of sharing, the consequences of which are seen as poor management.

This is one of the discomforts women feel. The idea of being alone and being in charge is often alienating. We are socialised into feeling connectedness through our roles in the family that often mean we are responsible for the maintenance of links. The thought of moving into a position of authority, which spells out to women that they must now go solo, is unfamiliar and discomforting to many.

There are legitimate reasons why there must be a point of responsibility within organisations, particularly formal ones. It provides for levels of accountability; ensures that things are done properly; that there is someone taking responsibility for certain tasks. In very hierarchical organisations this process often becomes subsumed into a culture of power that gives these positions an amount of prestige which creates distance from the subordinates.

Leadership is not the same as managing, although they sometimes overlap. Leadership looks outwards, managing downwards. Clearly there is a need for some points of responsibility, for arbiters of disputes and sources of quick decisions. The structures of families and the emphasis we have on them in social policy recognises that the dependent often needs an advocate with special responsibilities. These are skills required in workplace advocacy as well. We know we must have identified processes of accountability for good management. We also need to validate the roles of those who provide ideas and vision which excite and enthuse others to make changes.

The macho ideal of the upfront, progress-driven leader is often seen as more valid and prestigious than the good manager. One moves on and looks up, the other down. There is a perception at senior levels of the public service that management is the area where women are doing well. Their performance appraisals show high competency in managing people and tasks.

However, the leadership side—strategic planning and

creating visions for the future—is still seen within a masculine paradigm and can cause barriers when the most senior positions are filled. The established images fit with gender stereotypes which makes it difficult for women to break through. After all, they are being asked to take on the top position, and play it as a male game in more ways than one.

What we need to ask here is whether this hierarchy is necessary or even functional. Maybe components of the leadership role can be shared differently from the way they are today. It is rare to find a CEO who incorporates a balanced mix of ideas and good people management skills. Usually much of the work is actually done by less senior officers with the CEO setting the parameters. The question is whether the processes of management and planning need to be as hierarchical as they often are. New models of joint leadership/management teams with all members having the same status could be useful to explore.

How do we demasculinise the structure of senior management? We could create a feminised version of leadership, but not just by introducing the feminine; this change not only concerns individuals but also the way structures work.

Modern management theory suggests that the present hierarchies and Taylorised workplace—the command structures needed in factories—have gone. This makes it possible for women to develop a model of flatter structures which more closely reflects those that already exist in the community and in friendship networks. I do not include the family here. In earlier writings I have used the family as a model. However, it has built into it too many layers of hierarchy and power, and I believe the peer relationship models of friends and community are more appropriate.

## Cooperating leadership

In developing alternative forms for leadership, we need to look at the form most often identified with the women's movement. The collective was one of the optimistic inventions of the 1960s and 1970s. However, as shown in chapter 8, it often created as many problems as it hoped to solve.

The style of running refuges and other services by collectives was a reaction to the hierarchies of professionals and bureaucrats which operated the mainstream services, often leaving both consumers and women in lower rated positions out of the decision-making process. Interestingly, the critiques made by feminists back then are now widespread in current management literature, with an emphasis on flattening structures and the introduction of workgroups rather than command structures.

The collective was based on an ideal which was affected in part by the not-male analysis of early feminism: men have hierarchies so we will have flat structures. The other part of this was that as women were often in minorities in mixed groups, the pressure was on for a move from voting to consensus decision making.

One of the problems was that we were working within a paradigm where we assumed that equality meant sameness. The early collectives identified the internal hierarchies of various jobs: certain ones, mainly those mirroring male skills, were seen as prestigious, and others, often female ones, as more menial. In seeking to overcome this, collectives were set up on the principle of everyone sharing all tasks so the structures would remain flat. Few collectives survive on the basis of everyone doing everything, but have accepted that differentiating roles to reflect skills, interests and time available is essential if anything is to be achieved.

Problems came from wanting decision making to be consensual. By ensuring that everyone agreed on each point, it was believed that everyone would own the decision, and collective responsibility would be taken for its implementation. That was the theory, but it soon became obvious that the practice was quite different. Reaching consensus was too often a process of wearing down opposition, sometimes painful and very time consuming.

Despite these drawbacks, the collectives of the 1970s showed that cooperative flatter structures seemed to produce better outcomes. The concept of flattened structures is now appearing in writings by advocates of hardline economic reform and the downsizing of government. The current text book of the right, *Reinventing Government*,[3] has a chapter on reducing hierarchy and others on community managing. The authors' comments apply equally to other big institutions, and even some quite small ones which are non-government, although they tend to focus on the public service.

These critiques, from a variety of stances, suggest that a new management style, neither masculine nor feminine, is necessary. It would incorporate some of the best of the present system values, some alternatives, and some new ideas. We are part of a world which is rapidly changing and we need to develop new leadership structures to match it.

First, leadership should be seen as multifaceted. There are some supposed archetype tests which suggest one builds teams by combining particular types of people, for example, the Myers Briggs Type Indicators which are often used in job selection as well. The problem is that again there is a similar hierarchy of types to that of skills and these still reflect gender. We need to value skills, abilities and other qualities in ways which match their outputs and functions, not the gender or class, race or culture of their owners.

We must have the ability to deal with change because there are changes already happening that will make considerable differences to the way we live. We should be prepared to bring on reforms ourselves if others cannot see what is happening. To do so, and for more general reasons, leadership must become cooperative and supportive. Where is it written that there must be only one person at the apex? We seem to have taken on the idea of an isolated leader serviced by minions and advisers without question. It is probably a hangover from the good king, hereditary monarch concept, where loyalty to one lord was vital to maintaining the system.

Somehow in all of this we have not looked past the idea of the single leader. Also, the increasing complexity of both public and private sector senior positions has made management tasks themselves more isolating, as the hands-on action has been replaced by decisions made on even more distant briefings. Therefore boards and senior managers are often immured in their office suites with little contact with the world they are purported to be managing.

To effect change we have to unbundle some of this by looking at shared responsibilities and cooperative management. This would clearly allocate responsibilities but recognises that there are fewer hierarchies of skills than the present definitions indicate.

The dual components of vision and management may comprise top leadership, and placing them on the same plane would allow for joint leadership and provide support as well as broader input. I recognise that there is a need for authority and decision making at most senior levels, so this must be clearly designated as a role for one or another of the top two or even three managers.

As women in the Senior Executive Service of the Commonwealth Public Service are now working an average of twelve hours per day,[4] job sharing could provide two near full-time positions for workers who could remain human as well. Job sharing, at the top as well as below may reduce stress and the costs, and the pay levels offered to those in the private and even public sector would amply reward a scad of women and men replacing the top man.

### Not in the genes!

We do not need to retreat to an essentialist position of claiming that women would bring genetically programmed 'care' into top positions in order to justify our inclusion. The present macho, masculinity model of leadership is cracking quite severely because of its failure to deal with change.

What feminism can do, and is doing, is question the

assumptions behind existing structures and suggest alternatives. Some of these are not very different to those offered by more enlightened male groups. The flatter structure is already under way, the feminisation of senior management attributes has also started to take hold. This emphasis on people skills has been vocalised for many years but is slow to actually influence the selection of men, though it may assist women at senior levels.

This may also be a blind alley. Selecting women to remedy the deficiencies of men and still retaining a structure which leaves men on top solves nothing. The women selected will be those fitting the stereotypes, and masculine values will continue to dominate. We must make a change both in how leadership is perceived and in what it does. A supported and shared leadership concept involves staying in touch with other levels and having time for family and community. Women now in senior positions are desperate for this level of sharing and support as they are forced into time and structural models which are highly uncomfortable. To their credit, there are more and more men also questioning this model and moving out laterally.

We need to look at other ways of redefining leaders and in the process allow this to filter down. By breaking down the bureaucratic/management structure which sets individuals apart and does not expect those in senior positions to be included in daily life, we help to make leadership attractive and accessible at a range of levels. The onus of responsibility can be legitimately shared in ways which give us credit for skills and recognise diversity without hierarchy. Sharing the burdens and responsibilities also means sharing the fun of being effective.

What if we created an alternate view of community, based on the concept that we are all linked, not individuals competing with each other? This means that we would need to preserve the links that bind us and the common wealth. We must develop social policies and leadership which allow us to accept our responsibilities to each other and to the future as our first priorities.

The concept of consensus needs to be examined. One suspects that the confusion between consensus and groupthink (that is, finding genuine agreement versus suppressing dissenting views), has been part of the serious problems faced by Australia's governing bodies in the past. Differing views are not seen as valid, to be listened to and evaluated; instead the process takes over. Anyone offering differing views is squashed in the act of achieving harmony.

The dynamics of consensus politics are not designed to achieve the best content and are too often process oriented. They work from an assumption that there is a necessary equation between finding the best answers and that process by which agreement is achieved. By emphasising process, it negates the fact that differences require an examination of content. The opposition is seen as a problem, the opposer as spoiler, and the approval/belonging/linkages process is used to enforce conformity to an agreed norm, rather than a best fit.

Alternative views have to be acknowledged as part of the process of exploring options; diversity of experience should be encouraged as a vital source of differing views. In turn, these views should be respected, not just seen as a nuisance.

# CHAPTER 15

## Unlearning
## Helplessness

Moving from Other to Self, taking on responsibility for one's own actions, rather than expecting others to act for you, is not easy. It requires a mindshift at both an individual and structural level in the institutions we work in and which govern us.

In the recent controversy about the consequences of reporting acts of sexual harassment Helen Garner, in her book *The First Stone*,[1] illustrates how taking control can be misinterpreted. She is appalled at the consequences of a complaint against the Master of a university college. He loses his job despite being acquitted of claims that he sexually harassed two female students.

His innocence or guilt was not so much the issue for Garner. What she, and others, bemoaned was that the women failed to find a more direct response, a more definite and immediate way of dealing with unwanted attention than a very delayed report to the police. Why, she asks, couldn't these apparently self-confident young women have taken some immediate action to confront the Master directly and solve the situation in-house?

Garner herself knows this is not the answer. She tells of her reaction to the defence barrister's suggestion to one of the young women who laid the complaint that she could have slapped the presumed harasser's face. Garner goes on to reminisce about times when she politely ignored unwelcome advances, frozen into some form of feminine, good-mannered avoidance of trouble.

This theme is a constant one and the book highlights the dilemma that occurs when we expect girls to act in boy format; that is, to be able to respond to unwanted attention with an immediate, aggressive response. Expecting this reaction is unrealistic; girls are socialised into accepting blame for unwanted attention, into a feminine stereotype of non-aggression. The use of the law, when the college failed to act, was appropriate but misunderstood by many.

I remember very clearly a conversation with a school friend, when we were both aged maybe fourteen, on our way home from the pictures. Someone had whistled at us or commented on our appearance and she acknowledged the approach I ignored or rejected. The origins of the conversation have gone, but I remember my friend's rather shocking claim that she would politely acknowledge any comments made to her and about her.

This was quite unintelligible to me, as I had been taught a more aggressive response. One of the few practical things my father taught me in sub-adolescence was how to knee a man in the groin if necessary. If attentions were unwelcome, surely one either ignored them or responded rudely or aggressively. My friend, whose background was respectable, Anglo middle class, was adamant that her upbringing had taught her that she should answer politely, despite provocation. I found this sufficiently puzzling to remember over forty years later, and wonder about how we learn and unlearn passive reactions.

One of my starting points for this book was writing the Introduction to *Mother-Daughter Revolution*[2] by Elizabeth Diebold et al. The three authors identify the differences that develop in girls on adolescence. The move from active to passive is somehow tangled with hormones and the social. Their material is written in a context of social change, not personal and individual success. The three women are not selling personal growth but a recognition that mothers act as agents of social control and have to unlearn this.

Diebold et al raise the differences between Anglo/European young women and their Afro or Latino counterparts. The two latter groups are much more confident and outspoken in their teens and less likely to suffer from lack of a sense of self. The authors suggest that the racial struggles and in-built resistance protect these young women in some way.

While I have not dealt with cultural differences so far in this book I am very aware of them. As my own background is middle European and Jewish, I sometimes wonder if my 'differences' are not partly the result of this. My relatives were often upfront about what they wanted, even though my mother was more 'assimilated' into English manners and reactions. Is something transferred from the anglophone, mannered high culture to female popular culture which demands that young women are submissive and do not respond to aggression?

I remember that one of the first lessons I was taught when I was living in Italy in my early twenties, was to discourage unwanted attentions. 'Tell them *"Va fa'n cullo"* ', I was instructed by the locals. 'Then they will think you are a pro, not a tourist, and leave you alone.' Good advice and it worked, but many Australian women I shared it with found it very difficult, even in another language, to swear at bottom pinchers.

Passivity as a response to unwanted advances is learned helplessness. It should not be confused with a perfectly reasonable, passive reaction to advances from those with direct power over you, who are making explicit or implied threats by their actions. This is not blaming the victim but an attempt to explore whether particular Anglo cultures make valid anger and indignation taboo, or at least very difficult to express. Such a complex issue cannot be tackled only by individuals examining their own reactions; the need to toughen up our reactions and learn more counter moves and tolerance makes it a structural problem that should be addressed by the whole society.

Those taking the Diebold formula of encouraging young women to grow up confident and comfortable, because they and their mothers trust and reinforce their power, will not find it easy. They will encounter a social system which is likely to punish their non-conformity, and other women who find their confidence offensive. The institutions of media, education and politics will continue to promote models of feminine behaviour defined by traditional gender roles because they are still dominated by masculine perceptions of what should be.

### Creating authority

We women have to find ways of asserting our authority, of putting across the sense that we carry weight and that what we say must be taken seriously.

One solution, for some women, may be to fight back. There is a certain satisfaction in responding in-kind, as the film *Thelma and Louise* indicated. The cheers and excitement amongst the women in theatre audiences when the female protagonists blew up the truck owned by the lecherous male showed that many women do like to see the bitter strike! However, the reality is that women who do respond may be seen as reflecting the aggression of men, and are therefore likely to be disapproved of and rejected. There is little space for images of women who are not victims so it is no wonder we accept the passive templates so easily.

We should look carefully at words and actions that undermine the almost exclusively passive images of women. Being deemed perverse, difficult, aggressive, combative, outspoken, blunt, tough, forthright, trying, resolute and difficult, has to be understood in context. Without any of these labels male authority becomes difficult to enforce. If women are not seen and heard it is harder for us to influence change.

## What's mything?

Developing myths that give us a framework for leading and creating change is essential. The anthropologists, shamans, priests and elders of oral cultures recognised how myths acted as part of the normative cultures. The past can be used to create a legitimacy for the present, or to make the present seem very strange.

Some of the debates on history carry this element as a subtext. On the surface the arguments are about whether historian A is more accurate than historian B, but underneath the arguments are often about whose views and experiences create the past from which we work.

Feminist historians come under attack because they identify women and women's areas of interest which have been excluded from men's histories. A recent debate on World War II, for example, saw official historians defend their view of mateship and nationalism as being defined by battle; feminists brought in the examination of the war at home, the move of women into the jobs left by men and the social changes this wrought.

Organisational culture is now proving to be a much more resilient barrier than the formal, visible barriers we have mostly removed. Whether this is in the workplace, school, club or community, the types of behaviour that are seen as acceptable, the hidden rules, are proving much more powerful that the explicit ones we abolished.

When I run courses, I often involve participants in an exercise on delineating the rules of organisations in which they work or study. I usually start with clothes because most people are aware of what is and is not acceptable in certain settings. Dress codes are sometimes made explicit: sometimes uniforms are worn, at other times certain standards are set and conformity expected.

A recent lunch with some bigwigs, in summer heat, reminded me of the inappropriateness of some dress codes. As my taxi drew up behind a very expensive car, out climbed three men carrying their suit jackets; I was relieved that the taxi had been airconditioned as I was also garbed in a jacket. Inside, the presence of airconditioning and the formality of this gathering meant that it was essential for us to wear our coats. This amounts to a total rejection of commonsense in an Australian summer. We would save energy and costs by raising the temperature to a jacketless degree, but the masculine lore of formal suits overcomes the need for cost cutting, and women at these levels need to cover up to maintain their status and conformity.

In contrast, the welfare organisation I once directed assumed suits or stockings meant a funeral, court appearance or job interview. However, there are other areas of work where dress is a daily manifestation of proper behaviour. I remember one workshop where a senior women told of her discovery that her earrings were too loud. She dressed very conservatively but wore small but colourful ear-studs as a minor statement, and this was read as a failure to conform.

It strikes me that in changing the whole environment, the myths and the background noise are important ways of changing public opinion. The messages of daily control are powerful only when we accept them. As the following examples show, standards can be altered if they are challenged.

How did we change smoking from glamour activity to transgression and health hazard? The past decade has seen smokers become workplace, and often social, outcasts. They are now regarded as dirty health hazards rather than ultra-sophisticates. Similarly, the tax evasions of the 1980s, which became a national sport, are now seen as somewhat tacky. Considering that tax paying is easy to demonise, as people do not like paying tax, even a small shift is a significant achievement.

Given this, we should be able to devise strategies for presenting women with a wider range of myths and models.

Moving from passive to active can be done but it is slow and promoting this change can be expensive. It needs to work at many levels. We must ensure that the possibilities of alternate views are sufficiently comfortable and familiar, so people do not respond negatively to their manifestations.

This may mean that a few individuals go over the top, pushing the bounds of accepted female behaviour far enough to make the smaller changes of others seem reasonable. This is a version of the good cop/bad cop game. By letting some women be outrageous they catch the flak for others, and you achieve the change. These are what might be called the sacrificial ewes, the kamikaze women who make the new myths and push back boundaries. It is a difficult job that they may not even have voluntarily accepted, because by their actions they will be known and possibly rejected. They are the ones who first defy the dress codes, who talk about family in the workplace, who raise the issues of inadequate facilities for child care, who complain about being asked to do menial chores, who make complaints about the harassers and loudmouths.

It is not a lifetime role, and should not be left to one person alone. Change works best when the corporate culture is challenged by many. One may lead, or two or three, but if others back them, the changes will stick. Some women will fail, but they may find it easier to try again; others will be punished and isolated. Creating new icons, myths and models is not simple but it's necessary.

## Self-edging

Self-edging is a term I remember from school sewing classes. It describes the way material is woven so it does not fray or need hemming. While my main memory of learning to sew is of frustration, I developed a fondness for the concept of selvedges, as they are more often spelt. They need less fiddly attention and allow one to get on with producing the whole garment. I am using the term here as a metaphor for reorganising our boundaries so we can move on.

Leadership involves a knowledge of one's self as a basis for serving others, thus women need to work on understanding who we are. How do we know who we are? This is probably a crucial issue in terms of changing endemic low self-esteem in women. Men generally do not have this problem, so they feel less threatened when taking on leadership roles.

Leadership requires a positive sense of self, of knowing our boundaries and our linkages. You have to move into unfamiliar territory; to try something new if you are comfortable with your ability to make connections; to be seen and validated by others as someone worthwhile. Leadership and risk taking depend on being able to balance links and edges.

We all know of leaders who rely on the adulation of their followers, who use this constant reaffirmation as their fuel for self-acceptance. This is not an uncommon model. It results in populist leaders whose dependency on the good opinion of their followers mars their judgment. Whether men or women use this model is less important than acknowledging the problems that come from leaders who do not know their own value and limits. Our sense of self is tenuous if it is only based on how others see us, although we must be aware of how we seem to others, as this is how we realise the need to change or modify our actions.

We have to recognise the different ways in which women and men learn to determine who they are. Women are trained to do this by relating and men by their achievements, such as jobs and products. These experiential differences between male and female end up as gender-based identity markers. We all establish who we are in a range of ways but the mix differs between relationships with people and our use of attributes, skills and abilities.

We need to work out how we can ensure that girls as well as boys are praised for *doing* things: throwing a ball well, being good with their hands, excelling at things physical, manual and intellectual. The emphasis is on external acts, on proof of ability to do, and not so much on being able to relate. Being active is seen as gender appropriate for boys and should become so for girls.

We need to look at ways in which friendship models for boys and girls are different. Boys are presumed to be members of gangs or larger groups, which both compete and stick up for each other against outsiders. The basis for this is often group games where they learn to work together with mates. For girls, relationships tend to be based more on intense emotional linkages rather than action. We need both boys and girls to have options for different types of friendships and groupings so that these forms of socialisation no longer push each gender neatly into allocated roles as gatherer/housewife/mother, and hunter/protector/breadwinner.

While there are many tracts on developing assertion skills and self-esteem, most come from an individualised, psychology or New Age base. These assume that we, individually, need to make changes to ourselves and that if we fail to do so, or fail to succeed, we only have ourselves to blame. I am suggesting we need to look at much more systematic changes to the way we interrelate.

## Learning from men

We can learn from men, or maybe I will rephrase that to say there are characteristics associated with masculinity which are worth having. One sign of a maturing and dynamic feminism would be our willingness to recognise what we need to learn, as well as affirming what we know. The other side of this is the not-male syndrome, which is when women decry everything males do, or anything that is deemed masculine. It leads to the valuing of certain behaviours because they are not-male and condemning others because they are perceived as being associated with men and thus intrinsically bad.

This is both illogical and potentially damaging. If we reject some skills just because of their associations, we are engaging in sexism. Inverting the process still leaves women's choices dominated by male standards. We should look at the skills men acquire which may be useful for everyone. Think about the little girl who clambers up a tree or wall to see the other side, to test her climbing skills, to try her courage and suppress her fear. Do we react in the same way to her as to her brother? Evidence shows that girls are likely to be told to be careful, to avoid physical challenge in case of damage, or to be punished for putting themselves at risk. Boys are more likely to be seen as adventurous, daring or brave and are thus rewarded and encouraged. So girls learn to be cautious which, when we get older, translates into a fear of risk taking, particularly in the public sphere. This results in women avoiding speaking up, raising concerns or putting forward solutions.

This leads to the vexed question of what we can learn from men. Just as we may need to discard some of the behaviours that we have used to compensate for our lack of power, we must acquire others that will help us to use power effectively.

I want to look at some of the skills used to resolve conflict that will enable us to work together to achieve certain ends. These are the skills that men have. They are exhorted to play the ball not the 'man'; they learn that the goal is not to be loved or liked per se, but to achieve an end which will bring love, admiration and power. Such aims can result in an undue lack of concern for the way people may get hurt in the process but they also mean that goals are achieved.

What is the ideal mix if we want people to act as leaders? In the masculinity bag of tricks, boys are taught that it's the issues that matter and therefore winning and losing are not reflections of them personally. They depend on skills, resources and adequate briefings.

In femininity we are taught to monitor how people are

feeling, and that our role is to create comfort and happiness. Therefore we place these functions above outcomes. Neither the femininity nor masculinity models are adequate for what I would define as good leadership. This would involve an amalgam of what is taught to both sexes. Aspects of what men are taught would be useful for women to learn too. One problem is that these skills are seen as contradictory: if you are to be a task-oriented leader then too much concern for feelings will interfere with the outcome. Similarly, making people feel good is often seen as difficult enough without the additional tension of having to complete tasks within a set timeframe.

Leadership must deal with these contradictions. The hall-mark of good leadership is the ability to make choices between conflicting pressures and needs. In a way, this is recognised in some of the modern management books. They often outline what are considered female, people-based skills, which male managers are seen to have to learn. To acquire these skills it is believed that some additional learning is necessary to cover cultural defi-ciencies. Although management theory has recognised what is needed for men to supplement their existing leadership skills, it has not yet determined what is necessary for women.

Women are not seen to require remedial work in areas such as risk taking and conflict resolution. Instead, we do more work in male-designed management courses on areas in which we have already been trained in the home, or given advanced work in areas where we may have little grounding.

Let's look at what men know that would also be useful for women:

- An ability to make errors and survive to try again. Men tend to blame their tools or briefings when they make errors, rather than assume they are at fault. Women tend to blame themselves and therefore do not try again. We must learn by our mistakes and we need to keep trying.
- Solve the issues not the feelings. Men focus more on issues and can use debate to solve the problems. Women tend to deal with how people feel rather than the issues in situations of conflict.
- Face and resolve difficult situations. When something needs to be said which involves confronting another worker, for instance, women tend to put it off, because they hate being the one to cause distress or to be seen as the villain.

At first glance it would seem that these points could be easily corrected by some advanced form of assertion training, which deals with issues of conflict resolution. They are considered to be interpersonal skills that women will develop through training and practice. However, it's not so simple. Men learn these skills in a lifetime of socialisation because this is the script society writes for them. In varying degrees, men will conform to the stereotypes that are set for them. As a result of intermixtures of these with class, race and other predictors, some men will make it more readily into powerful positions.

The present social structure rewards with leadership roles, men who make it through that defined masculinity kit. It does not necessarily reward women for taking the same track and using the same kit. In fact, it excludes both men and women who fail to fit the stereotypes.

## Being heroic and bad

One of our major barriers to power is the prescription for women to be 'good girls'. We may have to change the definition of what a 'good girl' is to include elements of 'bad girl' traits as well. We must take on some characteristics of the angry and bad. Anger generally can either be seen as a legitimate reaction to injustice, or illegitimate if it ends in destruction and violence. However, this does not hold for women.

Gloria Steinem and Germaine Greer, in their post-menopausal discovery of life without the need for sexual partners, seem to see hormones as important. Both view their lives now as a time to reclaim the power they felt before adolescence, which allows them to be outrageous. What they seem to be saying is that they are prepared to do some of the acts defined as powerful and bad that they had avoided earlier in search of (male) approval.

I do not want to wait for women to finish with partners and child rearing before they are prepared to buck the stereotypes. Women need skills in dealing with argument, debate and, in particular, conflict. This statement is somewhat at odds with some present claims that women are more peaceable and will offer management all those inbuilt skills of emotional support and nurturing. These are dangerous claims because, as pointed out earlier, they pillory as unnatural women who fail to conform to the feminine stereotype.

In a study of top corporate culture Amanda Sinclair from Melbourne University,[3] identifies the executive culture as being dominated by certain norms, values and symbols. These are based on hero qualities and endurance in taking on and winning battles. Women are there as sirens/seducers or audience. She uses the myth of Odysseus (Ulysses), who was the ultimate wandering hero, as the image of executive man. His wife stayed home and avoided other men's advances by saying she would wait for him until she finished weaving a carpet. Each night she unpicked what she had woven that day while she awaited his return. Maybe this myth indicates the problem: he is too detached from his base, she is too concerned with maintaining it.

We assume that things have changed more than I suspect they have. After twenty years of public commitment to equality, I recognise that women are still treating each other, as well as being treated, as stereotypes and objects. We have added some new stereotypes but these are often constraining and reflect a new orthodoxy. Women as virtuous, women who abhor make-up, women as feminist heroines promoting what are seen as female virtues, may not be what women want now. By clinging to 1970s and 1980s images, or even by earnestly claiming difference by categories, we fail to recognise that progressive movements must do just this and move on. The lenses of the 1970s will not give us images of now and the future.

We need to create more varied images, including feminist images of power, both good and bad. A documentary on Leni Riefenstahl, filmmaker, portrayed how women like her who are defined as 'bad' are often overlooked. By all measures she was an extraordinary woman whose filmmaking showed an eye for images that has probably never been equalled. But her use of these skills was politically injudicious to say the least. Her relationship with Nazism puts her beyond the pale, but does it nullify her capacity and skills?

We need her and other 'bad' women as feminist antiheroes, as examples of superb skills but flawed morality. We do not see her in this manner as her political incorrectness disconnects her from the mainstream in ways that equivalent males are not. D.W. Griffiths is still admired despite his racist views in *Birth of a Nation*, and Riefenstahl's talent was equally superb.

## CHAPTER 16

# Taking
## Responsibility

I have heard many women say they would rather not have any-thing to do with the system as it is. If too many of us say this, we cannot make changes and life may become grim for everyone. Taking appropriate responsibility is one of the hardest lessons to learn. Women have tended to take on too much responsibility, but without the concomitant rights and power to implement change. Many women saw, and see, liberation as their right to choose not to take on the established female responsibilities.

As I write this, there is a debate on the radio about a statement issued by the Pope. His encyclical, *Evangelium Vita*, proclaims that women need to take up a new feminism. This new feminism, as defined by the Pope, means that women, who are 'particularly close to the mystery of life', have the special task to be guardians of life and its 'fruitfulness'. This is the late twentieth century version of the role of God's police, allocated to women in the early days of the Australian colony by Caroline Chisholm.

As a response to this conservative debate imposing respon-sibilities on women, feminist debate tends to focus on rights. In pushing to have more control over our lives, we have rejected the principle of duty-bound roles: women should stay with their husbands for the children's sake; women owe husbands their services and respect; women have a duty to care for older relatives, the infirm and the needy, and so on.

The new conservatives, now appearing in the USA, are nostalgic for a return to family responsibility: for 'family' read 'women'. Responsible women would reduce sole parenting, be home for the children, fulfill the husband's needs, maintain the relationships and reduce demands for State provision of services. But this formulation of women's duty and responsibilities is male driven. It is not what women have themselves freely chosen as their responsibility, either individually or as a group, but what some men in power decided were the elements of women's role within the male-defined couple.

The consequence is that feminists are often seen as opposing women's involvement in any traditional roles. There are now newer groups of women who claim they have freely chosen these roles, but also often demand that their choices be seen as warranting support from the State. Without casting any individual aspersions, I would question whether there has really been a fair debate on the relative merits of traditional roles, and whether these women have really been able to separate their views from the ingrained traditions of their mothers and grandmothers.

In pushing for the recognition of alternate views, I run the risk of alienating some women who do want to stay out of paid work. I restate, as I have often done, that this is a decision they have a right to make, as long as they have someone prepared to support them. They should not promote their choice as a better model of child rearing, nor claim that they are single handedly supporting the structure of the community, because the figures given later in this chapter suggest that they do not contribute more to the family than those who undertake paid work as well as caring for children and the home.

There are also claims made by women without paid work, or some of their public advocates, that they are looked down on by those in paid jobs. This is not borne out by a survey done in late 1994 by the NSW Ministry for the Advancement and Status of Women.[1] It showed that over 70 per cent of older women thought children were better off with mothers who are not in paid work. Of those with children, about half of those in paid work also thought that children were better off with mothers not in paid work. So women in paid employment still carry guilt, particularly as the rest of the survey indicated that few would opt to stay at home full-time even though they believed their children would be better off.

Women claim the need for empowerment, but this can only happen if we switch from taking on allocated responsibilities to determining our own. These should not be seen as individual decisions as they will always be made in the context of cultural and social mores. In most cases we are talking about social responsibility, broader than the circles and cycles of any one person or household.

Taking on responsibilities instead of having them thrust upon us is part of the process of leaving behind the victim, the martyr and therefore the angry, passive–aggressive role often played out by women who feel put upon. This does not mean we do what we want but that we share in the decision making about does what. By doing this we become participants in a social process of deciding who will take on the vital and important but not necessarily pleasant roles, including those of leadership.

At present, the assumptions are that so many tasks are so unpleasant, the only way that they will be done is to with coercion, rewards or pity. This ignores the variety of tastes we have, the possibilities of delivering the tasks in other ways, and the ability we all have to enjoy feelings of satisfaction for doing something for others that we would not necessarily want to do for ourselves.

Women have been allocated certain roles through a somewhat distorted process. No one could seriously believe that many of the tasks of domestic care are always pleasurable or tolerable. They are particularly difficult when we do them on our own. Housework is considered a service to others which is reciprocated with love and approval and, of course, financial support in many cases.

Carol Tavris, in *The Mismeasurement of Women*,[2] states that the concept of codependency can be equated with accepted stereotypes of female behaviour: servicing others, putting yourself last. The cure is masculinising and developing self-interest above all else.

What if we were to restructure domestic responsibilities so that they were shared; that those who enjoy them and want to do them should be rewarded by being paid and their skills recognised; and that those whose levels of incompetence were high or had distaste for the tasks would pay for the services of others? We should also recognise that some of these tasks are better done cooperatively and that the social interaction counters some of their repetitive and boring aspects. The pay rates must also be sufficient to ensure that those men and women who want to share in these tasks see them as both skilled and sufficiently financially rewarding.

At the other end of the scale, according to the current valuing of tasks, the apparently heavy responsibilities involved in leadership; the long hours, the pressure and stress that are claimed to be part of these roles, should also be shared more equitably. Once women distribute their gender-related tasks and responsibilities, so must men. As men find the pay rates and conditions sufficiently attractive to share the caring and domestic tasks, the working conditions at the top levels of management also need to change to incorporate women.

The sharing of duties and responsibilities will involve major shifts throughout society. These must be combined with changing some of the underlying assumptions about decision making and the criteria on which ethical and practical decisions relating to responsibility are based.

### Dealing with the domestics

Research shows that the major external pressures on women seeking to achieve more in leadership roles are the demands of family and household. Many women who take on powerful positions do not have responsibilities for spouse or children, others give up one or both as life becomes too hard to manage.

A study I did for the Women's Economic Think Tank[3] identified the similar contributions to the home and family made by women both in and out of the paid workforce. An examination of recent ABS time-use data indicates that women who combine full-time paid work with child rearing warrant most concern. They spend more than ten hours a day on their paid and family work tasks compared with less than seven hours spent by women not in the labour force. The extra time comes from having less time for sleep, personal care, leisure and social activities. Despite being full-time workers, they still spend two thirds of the time on housework that those out of the workforce spend.

Part-time workers spend more time on household work, child care and paid work combined, than do those full time outside the workforce. Their day is nine hours paid work and household work combined and they do 86 per cent of the family work that those at home do.

Looking at the three groups' contribution to voluntary work in the community, there is only two minutes per day difference between the contribution of those out of the workforce and those in part-time paid work. Women employed full time put in an average of 22 minutes and those not in the labourforce put in 31 minutes. However nearly half the difference in time was spent on religious activities, with the rest spread over helping other people.

These figures suggest that the extra contribution of women in paid work is often in addition to their housewife role. Therefore, there is no justification for claims from conservative groups that extra tax assistance should go to families with a member at home full time. The net benefit to the household is an estimated extra 90 minutes a day for household work, which would not seem to merit tax payer subsidies.

An analysis of ABS data shows that males do not spend adequate time on either housework or care of the sick.[4] Where there are women in the household, the time spent by men on housework is substantially less than that spent by women. The smallest gender difference is for non-family members where the difference is 20 per cent. The biggest difference occurs in families with children under fifteen where men do half the work that the women do.

Children under 15 add 132 minutes per day to household work for men and women in full-time work. For women out of the workforce, the presence of children adds 135 minutes to their daily housework on average. This suggests that the needs of children are adequately met by both groups and it is possible that as a result less time is spent on house cleaning, and that services such as take-away food replace home food preparation.

The point to note is that these tasks are not the sole responsibility of women, and certainly not of women at home. We all do some things for ourselves and most women do some things for others. Women in the paid workforce also do housework and nurture children. In fact, the differences as indicated by the time-use study by ABS[5] suggest that there is only about an hour's difference a day in housework and caring time between those working more than 20 hours but less than 35 and those not in paid work.

These figures show that the majority of women do housework; the majority of those with children take responsibility for their care; and women generally take part in community activities. Apart from the quantum of housework, there is little other difference in time spent as parent or community member. There-fore, I suggest that changes should be made in our domestic arrangements, as well as in the workplace.

## Doing without helpmates

Women are more likely to be locked into seeing themselves as helpmates, rather than leaders or producers. Remember the old aphorism which said 'behind every great (read successful) man there is a great (read supportive) woman'? This has been the consolation prize offered to women from time long past; that wives reflected and shared the power and glory of their hus-bands. This meant that although we were not expected to make it on our own account we could achieve through our association with a powerful man.

It is not so long ago that women were known not only by their husbands' surnames but also by their first names— Mrs George Brown clearly advertised her referred status. In the late 1970s, when I was the director of a major community organisation, we still had members who used their husband's name. I remember the embarrassment when one of my staff, who had no training in these niceties, referred to one female member on the phone as Stephen, and wondered at the chilly response.

As a young woman in the 1950s I was quite comfortable to be the girlfriend of a somewhat drunken university poet. It seemed to me more appropriate to sober him up for revue rehearsals and nurture his creative talents than to stretch my own creative wings. Similar situations were reflected in many novels, where the creative man had a patient wife who received her rewards vicariously.

This horrifies me now, but it seemed so normal even in the more radical bohemia we inhabited, a place where we scorned suburbia. I note with interest that some other well-known feminists emerged from the same group, the Sydney Push, including Germaine Greer. It appears we managed to go beyond the subordinate roles.

I recognised the same phenomenon some years ago when I read the diaries of my late stepmother. She was a world famous pianist, Hephzibah Menuhin. My father, whose mission was saving the world in some obscure way, demanded acolytes and constant reinforcement. He had managed to impose on Hephzibah, and an entourage of other women, the belief that his personal and sexual needs overrode their needs, often including her need to practise the piano.

Her socialisation as a child—as accompanist to brother Yehudi, as a female in a traditional support role—carried over into adulthood where she saw her role as supporter, not leader, and not even as solo pianist. She left no records of herself as soloist and wrote in a letter that she felt very uncomfortable in that role and preferred to blend into a larger group rather than being seen in any way as a leader.

This construct of femininity, particularly in partnering and coupling, is still a very powerful metaphor for women. The need to have a man as a signifier of one's value runs very deep. It is the basis of much of popular culture, the central matter of most soap operas and the basis of many myths and fairy tales.

While it takes two to partner, it does not seem to be as central to male identity. Men keep their name, and usually their jobs and careers come first. Even now after feminism has been with us for some time there are still relatively few women who retain or hyphenate their surnames after marriage. A small survey by some of my students at the University of Technology, Sydney found half the young women they interviewed on the subject of weddings wanted to change their names and even use the term Mrs, rather than Ms.[6]

This is not just a factor of education and job opportunities. I have seen many couples with tertiary qualifications, often marrying as students, where the husbands' careers have been the priority. The wives rear the children and follow their husband's trails as academics, diplomats or as corporate executives.

Many of those women are now in their late forties and fifties and when I have discussed their decision with them they are somewhat bemused at their lack of career success. While many are conscious of the choices they made, they manifest the privileges of referred status. Most of the women concerned have a level of anger and frustration at their lack of personal success, their sense of what could-have-been. This illustrates the problems of referred glory for many women; it is not really theirs so they cannot own it.

Men who receive this support have considerable advantages which allow them to pursue their careers with relatively limited responsibilities. Some conscientiously share child care and household tasks, because they are educated fellow travellers, but few would refuse a career opportunity, even if they felt it might deny their wives' options; the initiative would have to come from her.

In these cases it is the women whose sense of self was never clear enough for them to insist on having shared careers. Instead they lapsed into making their careers partially at least as wives of reasonably influential men. This is not surprising as they are following social prescriptions and avoiding the many risks involved in making their own stand.

The system is set for men to benefit from home-based support and the assumption is that this benefit carries through to the wives. A recent study in the USA[7] showed that men with stay-at-home wives increased their salaries ahead of those who had dual career families. The obverse of this is that there is no equivalent expectation available for women who very rarely have this level of support from their spouses. The few men who are prepared to take up the domestic support role are often seen as strange or unmanly. Occasionally when they do, they receive overly effusive support from other women as they are seen as making unbelievable sacrifices. The attention they get is focused on their nonconformity—it is never seen as normal for a man to support a women's career by forgoing his.

Of course men earn more, so there is economic logic in the pattern of men as the primary breadwinners when a choice has to be made. There are some strategies in place to narrow the gaps in pay rates but there is still the problem of women taking time out and reducing their hours of work so that they can maintain the household and support roles.

We have to acknowledge that it is not necessary to have a home support person if we want to encourage women to move into leadership positions. Men are not likely to move into the domestic support sphere, so the playing field should be flattened to remove the privileges of couples with one working.

## Valuing our home-derived skills

Acknowledging our own power and leadership potential requires us to look carefully at how we, and others, define skills and how they are defined for us. There are many skills we have developed in the home, family and community which stand us in good stead when we work as leaders. Many, under other names, are listed in the new management books as being vital in the workplace.

This section looks at some of the work we undertook at Distaff Associates, both in researching skills developed in unpaid work and in training women to recognise these. When we presented workshops for women on making career moves we stressed the importance of valuing their own skills. Three reasons were given for making a personal skill inventory:

1. Self-awareness: what do I know and where are the gaps?
2. Self-confidence: how to validate myself and define myself positively.
3. Self-promotion: presenting yourself to others in writing and in person.

I would add a fourth: developing a clear sense of the alternatives we, as women, can offer. This is about working within a framework or world view which includes and values the range of skills and experiences of the spheres left to women.

The following material comes from a project funded by the

Commonwealth Government's Women's Research Employment Initiatives Program (WREIP) to look at the skills women use in unpaid work.[8] With focus groups we explored the way women perceived skills. The findings show that some concepts of skills are sufficiently gender biased to militate against women's skills ever being recognised. The current hierarchies of skills, their naming and valuing, ignore or undervalue many which are developed through informal rather than formal learning. There is a disconcerting belief that unless something was learned in a formal course and certified, it cannot be defined as a skill.

This represents an extraordinary shift from the concept of trainee, intern and apprentice, which is still part of many training systems. These involve on-the-job training supplemented by formal learning, and rely on the idea that traditional learning involves a transmission from an expert to novice.

Our research started with the skills women develop doing unpaid work, which could be translated into paid workplaces, but took off in other directions. The real issue was not what types of traditionally-defined skills women acquired in households, but the often un-named skills women learned in managing households, community and human relationships. Much of this type of learning was transmitted by example, by 'learning on the job', and by exploring in supervised settings. It was learning about how to treat others, take care of feelings, and other rela-tionship-building skills.

This is gendered because it is women who tend to be taught more of these skills than men, who are often exempted from an early age as their tasks are to *do* things rather than to nurture people. Little boys are taught to promote themselves and be aggressive and little girls to care and manage emotions and clean up. These stereotypes move on through life and are reproduced contantly in paid and unpaid work structures.

What appears to be a relatively unacknowledged aspect of skill recognition are the words used to define it. *Skill* is not considered by most women to be a word that applies to much of what they do. Exceptions are those skills validated by certification or those involving the use of tools and machinery. On the other hand, activities which are often seen as female: communication, interpersonal relationships, ability to do many things at one time, to offer emotional and physical caring, and even the work of organising and producing material without machines, are not seen as 'skills' by women or men. When women do something well they call it 'natural', when they enjoy it they call it a 'gift', but as it is not seen as learned it is therefore not a 'skill'.

In the post-industrial society where higher numbers are employed in service industries than manufacturing, the type of workplace relationships which served the industrial revolution are now inappropriate. The concept of work teams as smaller, overlapping groups is regarded as more appropriate. These are closer to households, in the broader, old-fashioned sense, than assembly lines. Therefore there is a need to develop strategies and techniques for naming and rewarding the tacit skills necessary in these situations.

Our research indicates two major problem areas: that women are likely to substantially under-report their skills because of female non-recognition of the word; and that the workforce skill base is deficient because the defined 'skills' omit many which derive from female household experiences that are crucial to effective workplace functioning.

The assumptions underpinning the valuing of workplace skills are sufficiently flawed to ensure that the best intentions of the present process result in two unwanted outcomes: further disadvantages for feminised occupations as their skill base is undervalued and misrecorded; and the inhibiting of effective recognition of the skills needed in the workforce to deal with major changes in workplace requirements.

Many 'household' skills are relevant to areas opening up in communication technology, yet these cannot easily be translated into available workplace terms; for example, setting priorities, doing various tasks at the same time, sorting multiple inputs, as well as a range of skills in managing relationships which are required for effective work in groups. These skills are used daily in the workplace, and their use will increase as technology allows for a complexity of tasks to be performed simultaneously, with interpersonal skills necessary for organising workloads.

The good secretary/personal assistant needs many of the skills learned in the household and community. Advertisements for a 'mature' person often obfuscate what is wanted: an effective office housewife able to deal with complex tasks while also doing the emotional housework.

Women who bring these skills into the workplace are not good advocates of their own areas of expertise. It is possible that this, in part, is a consequence of our need to be accepted in the workplace on masculine terms. By trying to avoid office hand-maiden roles, women sold themselves short. We tried too hard to look at paid workforce roles through the existing paradigms and avoided anything that smacked of wifely duties. In the process we closed off the possibilities of recognising that changing workforce requirements could validate the importance of different skills.

I propose then that we learn something from the current revolution in the community sector, that is, that productivity is increased when people work cooperatively in groups. Therefore we should reorganise household life as well as the paid workforce to limit the solo performance of duties. This suggests that the private and public be melded in ways which both recognise our needs for space and privacy but also place limits on this.

Management courses are beginning to acknowledge that people are the core, not machines, and that people skills and strategic planning are essential. The language of corporate planning comes from the military but there are fewer generals than housewives, and the ability to juggle time and resources is practised more at home than it is in the jungle!

Many of the methods used for evaluating jobs derive from systems that were based on assembly line models. Jobs were defined in relation to the manual or production process where tasks tended to be individual and repetitive. When this is translated into non-assembly line processes the initial framework is often overlaid with 'other' aspects relating to autonomy and to levels of supervision of other staff, or to the conceptual skill levels of intellectual work.

Skills ratings generally still relate to the individual worker and what are deemed to be his (*sic*) tasks. Jobs are not seen as part of an interactive process until the issues of management are raised at more senior levels. This assumption that interpersonal skills are only to be seen as valuable when they relate to the use of hierarchically designed power structures, runs counter to current moves towards work groups.

In community and household groups the ability to work with others, to be members of teams and to take responsibility for parts of what is seen as a whole, are supposedly valued. What we need to state and prove is that these are skills we have learned, and therefore are neither universally held by women, nor do they come with the genes. Developing them to a high level can be valuable and valid and needs to be recognised as crucial to improving workplaces and leadership.

The women we spoke to in the research groups often assumed their 'skills' to be natural and therefore they required no effort and should not be rewarded. This again is a peculiarly feminine response which indicates the low level of esteem these attributes are allocated because they are home related and female. A self-taught carpenter would not be as modest about their product as a self-taught home cook.

Think about the gender divisions of hunter-gatherers. The gatherers provided the great bulk of food but hunting was more prestigious. In many cultures the rituals of hunting were the public face of power but the collectors of food and water were the major contributors to well-being and survival.

Who defined the paid workplace as the real world, the

important one which had to be supported by the household? How is it that the objective for living appears to be the paid workplace and the economy? Why is the relatively structured and organised workplace seen as more demanding than the chaos of home settings? Who sets the criteria and on whose behalf?

Women have had our accepted spheres devalued and overlooked and have been told the hard work is out there somewhere away from the home. I know this is wrong because I find it easier to make policy than make a bed. There are many times when the chaos of relationships, emotions and the attendant chores are all too scary and I rush to a meeting with relief that the relationships there are institutional and formal.

I had a father who saved the world as a serious alternative to washing up. He was never available for either physical or emotional housework because his time and skills belonged to a wider world and there was no time for the trivia of cleaning or cooking. It took me years to see how convenient this was, and neither of his wives ever realised it. The problem was not that he would not or could not do it, but that he was convinced that his skills and work had to take precedence over anything else and that other tasks were suitable only to minions. This was a clear example of gender differentiated skill values, one I relate to in a way because I am a poor housekeeper, with limited ability and patience. The difference between father and daughter is that I appreciate and value the skills that make groups work, make households work and produce order and comfort.

Remember the example of the division of labour in many

two-income households described earlier: the man leaves home at seven in the morning as he has work to do; the woman is left with dressing two small children, putting the clothes in the washer, pulling the dinner ingredients from the freezer, finding bunny ears for the Mad Hatter's tea party and cooking a batch of Anzac biscuits for a fund raiser at the child-care centre, before making it to the relative peace of her workplace.

Who displays the greater skills? This example shows not only how men get away with this lifestyle but how women are part of the process. It is our complicity and undervaluing of what we do that this chapter seeks to highlight. If we are confident that the skills we use are also worth rewarding we can begin to reframe the process. Not everything we do, as women, is valuable: if someone is a bad cook, and fails to communicate with the family and maintain good relationships, her time spent on these tasks cannot be regarded as skilled or productive. There are differences between the abilities of those who can patiently and carefully provide good personal care for children, the aged or someone with a disability, and someone who just manages to do what needs to be done.

Women need to recognise that some of us have very advanced skills in people management, building relationships and caring for others. The corollary is that some of us are poorly skilled in the areas we are allocated. By recognising our failures, we can enhance our successes.

# CHAPTER 17

## Some Immodest Proposals

The essence of leadership is making up your own mind and then being able to take other people with you. Because of this I wondered how appropriate it was for me to make suggestions about possibilities for the future. At times throughout the book, I have indicated where I stand politically and some of the values I hold. This chapter also, inevitably, reflects my beliefs.

I have made suggestions here specifically on the grounds that I believe they are necessary, but not sufficient, preconditions for leadership. Leading women, if they are to offer variations from the present companies of leading men, need to be drawn from a wide spectrum of household and family arrangements. If women with children and family responsibilities are almost always seriously limited by these, then those currently in power will not have the personal experience necessary to represent these overlooked areas.

We should, therefore, carefully examine the way we structure our households, our attitudes to housework and the care of others, and the social and physical barriers to change. We should investigate the political and commercial options for developing alternate ways of delivering household services and society's will to put these in place.

This does not mean we should adopt entirely masculine assumptions that nothing done in the home is of sufficient value to be accounted for. Production and consumption in the home cannot be disregarded. We need more discussions on how unpaid work should be acknowledged and who should be responsible for it.

So here are some proposals.

### Mixing the balance: paid work, community and family

A balance is necessary in life. To achieve this we must move away from broad definitions of workplaces as functional and households as emotional. Similarly, home, the haven in a heartless world, as defined by men, cannot be used by them as an antidote to the workplace's discomforts and demands, if this means having a wife as servicer. Family care must be distributed more equitably.

We have to recognise that the validation of identity comes both through relationships we have and what we produce. Earning money and living by independent means, for example, are markers we all need.

Men, as well as women, must strive for a balance of experience. Masculinity, defined as requiring the ability to act physically or mentally but excluding anything too emotional or nurturing, currently denies men this balance. Their ability to care is seen as inappropriate for everyday use, and a lack of desire for power or promotion are seen as signs of inadequacy.

## Recognising workplace identity

The workplace is not regarded as part of the community in western capitalism, though small business and the more feudal Japanese models do recognise it as such.

Those in the workforce need to consider relationships and their need for personal affirmation as much a part of their function as production or service delivery. This is increasingly relevant as we move towards more service-centred industries, and it is recognised in the emphasis now placed on people and communication.

## Permeating the work-family boundaries

It is necessary to create permeable boundaries between home and workplace. We have had considerable debate on family-friendly workplaces, and there are some signs of this debate being recognised, for example, in the form of parental leave and flexible and part-time work. Also a few employers have some form of child-care or elder-care assistance. However, most of these benefits assist you to be either at work and fully involved or not there at all. There are few moves which acknowledge that you can carry your family needs into the workplace.

As a starting point, we must remove the taboos on using the phone at work to organise and even deliver care and maintain the household. With no one at home, some domestic arrangements have to be made at work, particularly if you are employed full time. Telephoning from work does take time but we also often bring work home in our heads, and occasionally we may be able to work at home.

## Outsourcing household services

We must move from assumptions that the family can or should perform the bulk of household tasks and instead look at ways to create more congregate provisions of both social and commercial services.

Feeding children at school and in child care and feeding adults at work would help to make the evening meal a more pleasant, less time-consuming task. Encouraging local, cheap and nutritious food services where one can eat out is another.

We should validate the development of neighbourhood cleaning and laundry services staffed by groups of people who can deal with a mass of tasks in tandem and provide these cheaply while earning a living. We need to accept these services as a norm for the family and not as some form of cop-out or consider them to be exploiting others.

We need to see child care as the standard and the women who keep their children at home as the exception. Our concern should be for those children whose experiences are limited to those which one or two parents can offer. We need also to ensure that good support services are available for people with restricted capacity for self-care and mobility. These should allow them to take part in the community, not be restricted to home and a single carer.

None of this negates the need to change the workplace so

that management of the household can be combined with paid work.

## Child care

The hours of work and child care should be geared to allow both parents to mix unpaid and paid work, play and community activities. Why should fathers miss out on the joys and travails of child care, and the children have fewer hours of fathers? While this time may be available for men in lower level positions and when they deliberately opt out of high pressure jobs, it should be available to all. What I am proposing is a general move to shorten working hours, particularly for those with family responsibilities, both men and women.

We need to make it generally understood that it is inefficient to consistently work long hours. We must also change the workplace culture which demands the total commitment of workers, even at senior levels. This situation is not socially or economically efficient and it disrupts the balance of domestic and community life. Such changes must come from all levels, as reform is always an up and down process. Without change in the personal, the political will not work; without the political, the personal is not enough.

## CHAPTER 18

# Home is a Poor
# Quality Workplace

The industrial revolution created a division between public and private. It moved paid work into factories and out of the house, and left households with the residual responsibilities which were the continuation of the community. Households grew smaller and more socially dysfunctional as the size of families, the structure of cities and the location of workplaces changed.

The survival of the unregulated relationship of family and community was assured by the gender divergence of roles. The caring and maintenance of relationships which created and maintained the community were separated from paid work and public, State activities and were defined as women's work.

The market workplace and the money it offered became the focus for the assessment of skills and status: what you did became more important than who you were. The education system and credentials were increasingly geared to production of workers as a group and not the person. Therefore, it is not surprising that the workplace became the source of identity and relationships with workmates often replaced those with neighbours and friends.

Within this development, the concept of family and household was not only devalued but gutted of much of its meaning.

The major production roles of families were replaced by the consumption role as ready-made items produced outside replaced homemade goods. The size of families decreased and neighbourhoods became places of strangers rather than communities. The postwar baby boom locked women in homes with ideology and nappies. However, the inexorable move of women back to paid work in the 1960s suggested that the household had limited hold.

The pill and technology reduced the pressure of child care and housework. Women still filled their days but the tasks were often derived from increased demands on standards rather than the necessities of maintaining health and providing care. Such tasks were no longer fulfilling. In the 1960s, Betty Friedan[1] named the discontent of housewives 'the condition that had no name'. Through recognising what was happening to women, the women's movement was created. Women entered positions of paid employment in increasing numbers, but still carried their household responsibilities and their guilt.

## Abolish housework!

We need to recognise that the industrial revolution has been followed by the purchase-of-services revolution. The demand now is for those services that replace the need for household work, and this is one legitimate way to look at the redistribution of this type of work. This does not mean the household is a form of workplace which is admirable or should be used as a model for other activities. The modern urban household is neither an effective nor an efficient provider of care from an adult's, nor most probably from a child's viewpoint.

The results of time at home for most women is a diminution of self-confidence and self-esteem, regardless of whether they were in high or low-powered jobs prior to having children. It could be seen to be an almost inevitable result of spending too much time on your own with a small person who has only limited communication skills.

If we acknowledge that we are social beings, we must recognise that our sense of self comes, in part, from our connections to others and the way others see us. Kith and kin: our circles will vary in the importance we put on parents, children, partners, other relatives, friends, strangers, neighbours, workmates, and community contacts. The mix will depend on how we spend our time. We will sometimes have close relationships with people with whom we have little contact, we will see others daily or weekly, we will have intense relationships with some people, or maybe just a few. Some of us may have many less intense relationships, others fewer but stronger ones.

Women at home do not have the opportunity to develop and maintain varied relationships. The relations are often scattered and connections are made by telephone and car. There are few people home during the day in most neighbourhoods and the majority of households are in suburban areas, not close to workplaces or even shops. Therefore, the opportunities to maintain face-to-face contact with other adults are often limited.

Our sense of being is closely tied to these meetings. For many people the workplace has become a place of intense contacts. We spend many hours there, sometimes more hours than we spend awake at home. What happens to those of us with paid jobs affects the way we feel about ourselves. The respect we receive, the sense of value we gain from both the tasks done and the recognition it brings, all add to our sense of self.

The community activities some of us find time for also provide us with a sense of who we are and how we are valued. These might also come from our children, our interests or our social and political obligations, and involve us in formal and less formal processes with others with common interests. Sometimes study or hobby activities also offer roles and identities we may value. While women not in paid work have more time for these, the evidence from time-use studies is that their participation in these spheres exceeds those in full-time work but not those in part-time work.[2]

Activities which carry within them certain images for participants, whether they be travel, holidays, attending the theatre or playing sport, for example, also contribute to the way we believe others see us. When I do something that I both enjoy and I know other people enjoy, such as going to the theatre or a concert, I feel good about myself. All these activities involve a reasonable level of interaction with other adults, both in the doing and in the conversations about them. They are about being in a community of adults, belonging and being seen to belong. These are all parts of the self we develop through our connections with others.

Yet the world has changed. For the first time ever we see women at home with maybe one or two children, having few, if any, other daily family or community contacts. This has created a situation in which women are deprived of adult contact for many hours, even days. Like prisoners in isolation, we can go stir crazy. The lack of indicators of who we are and how we are seen by others leaves us the task of self-affirmation. As women we have not been trained into this process so we rapidly lose what sense of self we may have had in paid jobs or school and develop a feeling that we are being only for others.

### Free the children!

Over the past decades, some women have clung furiously to motherhood and housework as the only way to affirm their power. The rhetoric of child rearing has maintained that this is the appropriate place to be and failed to deal with the changing nature of home-based child care. Yet too many of these same women, when asked what they do at home, will answer 'nothing' because the work seems to them to be never-ending and insignificant.

I have run group after group with women doing skills audits and career planning and heard this description of their time out of paid work. Even when women move back into paid work or adult company in unpaid community groups, they feel their lack of self-value creeping up on them. When we researched women's unpaid work in home and community[3] the overwhelming response was that this was not of value to the world outside, nor, when pressed, to themselves.

This is a contradiction which I have noted over the years. The women who most furiously and publicly defend their home-based role seem, at another level, to be dubious about its value.

The noise they make is almost in inverse proportion to the confidence they have that what they do is worthwhile. Therefore they aggressively demand a public valuation of it.

This is, I suspect, the effect of the isolation of adults from other adults. In child rearing texts the emphasis on family qua mother as primary carer implies that one adult to a child is somehow acceptable. However, there is increasing evidence that this is neither desirable nor natural as both children and mothers are likely to suffer the consequences of poor socialisation and sociability.

The converse of this is the assumption that the care provided in the home is the norm and can be the optimum. It is rare to see out-of-home care touted as possibly inherently better than the home-based service. The common assumption, typified in recent claims by Penelope Leach,[4] is that children are best reared by mothers with only limited outside input. There are always studies being done to measure the supposed ill effects of alternative care, which is assumed to have to measure up to the presumed benchmarks set by maternal care.

What if we started from the quite reasonable assumption that the present child-rearing unit of one adult with one or two children, plus part-time assistance from another, is itself inadequate? Why should we assume that one adult can meet the needs of one or two children? What is our yardstick for measuring the performance of the so called ideal type?

It does not exist. Is there a common equation of child-rearing models with what is assumed to be a universal, natural model? Again, this model does not exist, and if we did draw out common themes from the variety of ways children are reared there is not even a constant on mother care. The theory that a mother in attendance is sufficient unto itself is not borne out. Children are reared in a wide range of models, most of which involve far more adults and children than are in a nuclear family.

Therefore, it is a reasonable assumption that the present family unit is too small, variable and fragile to offer good child rearing to the majority of children. The limited adult availability puts too much emphasis and stress on the mother. Many women recognise this so they use their time to seek out other adults and children to mix with at play groups or informal care groups.

We should look at using child-care services as a natural and integral part of child rearing. A child in a care centre can find a range of adults, children and activities; the social contacts that were once available within the household. Group care teaches children to relate to many adults and children. Also, they are protected against too intense and limited relationships with one or two adults, which may also be less than satisfactory. Through group care, children and adults retain a better sense of them-selves, anchoring this in the reflections of multiple relationships, something the children need to become sane, whole adults.

What if we look at children who do not receive some form of child care away from their mothers as deprived? And what if the assumption that the care and nurture which all children need can all be provided by one person is spurious?

John Irvine, a child psychologist researching children's play, often sees children in a clinical setting who have been play deprived, and who need to be released from over-control so they learn to interact. This raises the issue of how people-deprived children can become in the smaller households and families. He identifies a lack of joint play between parents and children and discusses the types of toys and activities parents and children can share. But he does not take the next step and question whether adults are the best people to play with young children. This sets up the possibility that the efforts of both parents, even in carefully designed quality time, cannot and should not be seen as the major or even primary mode of providing play and experience for children. If children are in some form of care for part of the week, they will have many experiences of informal and directed play with peers, and with adults other than their parents.

Gay Ochiltree, in a review of a range of studies on the effect of child care on children,[5] comes to the conclusion that there is no evidence of harm. In fact she finds that the reverse is probably true; that is, that child care in congregate groups may provide clear benefits for children. She outlines the differing types of socialisation that mixtures of family care and group care can contribute to what she names as 'parallel socialisation'.

These two experts put a good case for the use of out-of-home care to offer children experiences that are difficult to obtain in the small family unit. There are, of course, issues of the quality of care but these issues also exist within families. Children with more than one form of stable care are less likely to be damaged by poor care from any one source, whether parent or other carer.

There are reasons for discouraging continued home-based

support systems for people in leadership positions. Many women married to male leaders complain that they have essentially raised children on their own. The case of Hazel Hawke vis à vis ex-husband Bob, is a public illustration of the absent father, of de facto sole parent roles. This situation does neither the children, the mothers, nor ultimately the leaders any good.

## Caring without compulsion

Similarly, assumptions should not be made about home-based care being the best option for the frail, people with disabilities or others who require ongoing assistance with daily tasks. The de-institutionalisation movements over the past decades have often assumed that normalisation involved family care. This ignores the needs of almost everyone, including the person requiring care, to have broader interactions and choices than most homes can offer—the needs of the supposed caree are often not considered in assumptions made about the carer.

We also confuse contiguity and care. Being there to provide occasional care, security and supervision may not be necessary. With new technology there are many options for maintaining contact and gaining urgent assistance. The study of telephone use by women,[6] revealed how much care can take place over the phone lines. Women not only manage many of the household tasks from the workplace, but also offer a level of care and support to the elderly and frail by the same process.

## CHAPTER 19

# Strategies
# for Success

In this final section we look at some of the ways we, as women, can move as individuals and in groups, to make our own way and to encourage others. The strategies we have to develop are threefold: attaining positions of power; being there in numbers that can initiate change; and making changes. In conjunction with these we must analyse the way we see ourselves, how we socialise our daughters and sons, and the way we take part in organisations. Think about your life in the community and the workplace. Here are some starting points for you to consider.

## Taking on positions of authority

- Run for president or chair; this can be in your job, in the community or in your leisure activities. Go for the top position; it is often less work than the secretary's and more influential.
- If you are on committees, don't just sit there quietly. The talkers do not know more, they just talk more, so put your views forward. Give other women your public support, when appropriate, even if you feel that you may be on the losing side. Losing is not a contagious disease but do try to work out how to win the points next time.

- If you want to get something done, do it. Work out how to and find others to work with you. Don't assume that you can't do it, or that someone else should or will do it.
- If there is a job going for which you are qualified, don't wait to be asked to apply, put yourself forward.
- Don't wait for others to notice you are good at something; make sure it is noted and not overlooked.
- If you are the leader, use the position wisely but do not try to pretend you are still one of the girls and put yourself down or abrogate your authority.

### Putting women's views

- Put your views forward, and do so without apologising or modestly waiting to be asked, particularly if men are freely offering theirs.
- Check how many men put their views forward in a discussion vis à vis the women and how often they speak and make sure the women match them.
- Validate what you know and use it with authority.
- Remember that men often talk about things before they know everything there is to know and you should too, but we should also acknowledge that there is more to learn.
- Don't wait for someone else to start the ball rolling; start it yourself when you can.
- Don't be put off if men say you talk too much or are too aggressive. The male threshold for women's participation is very low.
- Remember all the women who say nothing, and instead, try to

make sure that women's voices are heard, even if you have to talk quite a lot to compensate.

- Don't just say what is wrong, go to the next step and suggest how to fix it.

## Supporting other women and surviving yourself

- If you lose a point or issue, try not to take it personally, be devastated or feel rejected. The opposition is probably against what you said, not you personally.
- Don't believe that you have to deal only with people's feelings and make them feel better. Sometimes you have to be able to disagree and sort out differences and conflicts. You are not their mother.
- Don't play victim in order to get people to do things.
- Don't be too shocked or hurt if it is other women who put your efforts down, and remember this can come from both radicals and conservatives.
- If you can't do something yourself and other women try to tackle the same problem, don't punish them if they approach it differently from the way you think they should.
- If you feel angry with a powerful woman, make sure you are not judging her more severely than you would a man who does the same thing.
- Don't expect your problem solving to work all the time or even most of the time, as long as it works sometimes.
- Enjoy at least some of your power and keep a sense of humour.
- Make sure there are a few others with whom you can joke and grieve; spend time with your peers.

• Expect negative reactions from others; they are a measure of your effectiveness.

One of the hardest lessons to learn is how to cope with conflict, hostility and disapproval. Someone recently made a comment that boys' playground games teach them to lose and to obey, as well as to win. Girls often abandon games which cause conflict because they see developing relationships as more important. Men will expect you to take criticism their way and for your own survival, you need to learn the rules, even if ultimately you want to change them.

## Policing the possibilities

Policy and politics now deal primarily with what are defined as public issues. Within them is a hierarchy which positions the economy high and community services down low. Ignored too often are the private spheres, the areas of community, family, personal relationships, pleasure, environment, culture, sharing, giving and being; in fact most of what we really live for. A shift in both the content and process of public policy is therefore essential.

I want to raise the possibility of moving towards a future which is more concerned with people, not the bottom lines of accounts; where the main attention is on social capital and goals, and economic means are regarded as just one of the ways of achieving these; where quality of life is not seen just in terms of material wealth but in relationships and public good. To do this we need new ideas, creative energy, ability to see past the present limiting barriers and a commitment to passing our children a more optimistic future than the present.

In my Boyer Lectures[1], I explored the concept of social capital, the totality of the social linkages that offer alternative views of the world to current dominant macho frameworks. I raised the question of whether social capital and cooperation may be better social and economic indicators than competitiveness. I am proposing a truly civil society based on trust and reciprocity, which also values dissenting voices.

There are now many writers and commentators asking questions about other ways of seeing the community and society, so the possibilities for new ideas are there. My views are one script for a feminist utopian road movie; put yours into the picture!

# Endnotes

### Introduction

1 Carmen Lawrence in a speech to the United Nations Association in 1994.

2 Leonie Still has written widely in this area, see *The Career Patterns of Enterprising Women: a comparison of executives and entrepreneurs*, Westmead, NSW: School of Business, Nepean College of Advanced Education, 1987.

### Chapter 1

1 See G. Dougray, *The Executive Tart and Other Myths*, London: Virago Press, 1994.

2 See J. Mills, *Womanwords*, London: Virago Press, 1992.

3 See Hester Eisenstein, *Contemporary Feminist Thought*, Sydney: Allen & Unwin, 1984.

4 A. Bullock and O. Stallybrass, *Fontana Dictionary of Modern Thought*, London: Fontana, 1977.

5 Max Weber, *The Theory of Economic and Social Organisation*, New York: Oxford University Press, 1947.

6 For further discussion of Foucault's concept of the ownership of power see J. Sawicki, 'Foucault and Feminism: towards a politics of difference', in C. Pateman and M.L. Shanley, *Feminist Interpretations and Political Theory*, Oxford: Polity Press, 1991.

7 B. Caine and R. Pringle, *Transitions: new Australian feminisms*, Sydney: Allen & Unwin, 1995, p.xi.

8 ibid, p.xiv.

9 A. Hede, 'Personal Communication', an unpublished paper on management and leadership carried out at the University of Queensland, 1994.

10  H. Garner, *The First Stone*, Sydney: Picador, 1995.

11  Here I am referring to Helen Garner's public reading at the Museum of Contemporary Art, Sydney, 23 May 1995.

## Chapter 2

1  Ann Oakley is the author of a number of books, including *The Captured Womb: a history of medical care*, New York: Blackwell, 1984, and *Becoming a Mother*, New York: Schoken Books, 1980.

2  Rebecca West, as quoted on the back cover of Susan Faludi's book *Backlash*, London: Chatto & Windus, 1992.

3  For examples of this see the works of Hobbes, Rousseau, Plato, Locke, Durkheim, and Parsons, amongst others.

4  See C. Pateman, *The Sexual Contract*, Cambridge: Polity Press, 1988.

5  See R. Titmus, *The Gift Relationship: from human blood to social policy*, England: Alden and Mowbray, 1970.

## Chapter 3

1  M. Gross, *Sydney Morning Herald*, 5 October 1994.

2  J. Margo, *Sydney Morning Herald*, 13 October 1994.

3  Max Weber, *The Theory of Economic and Social Organisation*, New York: Oxford University Press, 1947.

## Chapter 4

1  See *The Australian*, 9 October 1993.

2  D. Ironmonger, *Australian Households: a $90 billion industry*, Discussion Paper no. 10, Centre for Applied Research on the Future, Melbourne University, Parkville, 1989.

3  I. Porter, 'Managing Manager Management is Now the World's Most Challenging Challenge', *Australian Financial Review*, 20 September 1994.

4  See *Australian Financial Review*, 20 September 1994.

5  World Competitiveness Report, compiled by the United Nations, 1992.

6  J. Clout, 'Shake Up in the Classroom', *Australian Financial Review*, 25 August 1994.

7   Conference proceedings of *Women, Power and Politics: an international conference to advance the rights of women and their role in politics*, Adelaide, 8–11 October 1994. Published by the Women's Suffrage Centenary Steering Committee, Department of Arts and Cultural Development, Adelaide, October 1994.

8   Australian Bureau of Statistics, *Labour Force*, Canberra: Australian Government Publishing Service, December 1994.

9   See Adele Horin's article on research done by C. Brown at the Southern Cross University in *Sydney Morning Herald*, 17 January 1995.

10  See, for example, studies by Deakin University, Dallas Isaacs and Marilyn Poole.

11  C. Lindblom, 'Still Muddling, Not Yet Through', *Public Administration Review*, no. 36, 1979, and frequently anthologised.

12  A. Sinclair, *Trials at the Top*, Melbourne: Australian Center, Melbourne University, 1994.

13  See *The Australian*, 18–19 February 1995, p. 29.

14  See *The Australian Magazine*, 18–19 February 1995.

### Chapter 5

1   For examples of this see the works of Hobbes, Rousseau, Plato, Locke, Durkheim and Parsons, amongst others.

2   H. Lynch, 'Breaking Through the Glass Ceilings: women in big business', in *Women, Power and Politics*, Conference Proceedings Adelaide, 8–11 October 1994. Published by the Women's Suffrage Centenary Steering Committee, Department of Arts and Cultural Development, Adelaide, October 1994. pp 168–178.

### Chapter 6

1   H. Garner, *The First Stone*, Sydney: Picador, 1995.

2   Anees Jung has written widely, her most recent book is *Unveiling India: a woman's journey*, New Delhi: Penguin, 1987.

3   Here I am referring to a term used by Caroline Chisholm and taken up by

Anne Summers in her book *Damned Whores and God's Police: the colonisation of women in Australia*, Victoria: Penguin, 1974.

4   In B. Caine and R. Pringle, *Transitions: new Australian Feminisms*, Sydney: Allen & Unwin, 1995.

5   There is evidence to suggest that sex differences operate as a variable when considering causal attribution of success and failure. See McMahon, J.D. (1971), Shibley Hyde, J. (1991).

## Chapter 8

1   J. Mills, *Womanwords*, London: Virago Press, 1991.

2   ibid.

3   J. Freeman, 'The Tyranny of Structurelessness', *Ms Magazine*.

4   See C. Chisholm, *Emigration and Transportation Relatively Considered*, 1847.

## Chapter 9

1   M. Garber, *Vested Interests: cross dressing and cultural anxiety*, New York: Harper Perennial, 1993.

2   F. Fanon, *Black Faces, White Masks*, New York: Grove Press, 1967.

3   S. de Beauvoir, *The Second Sex*, New York: Bantam, 1952 (original publication 1949).

4   Discussion paper prepared by the National Council for the International Year of the Family, March 1994, *The Heart of the Matter: families at the centre of public policy*, Canberra: Australian Government Publishing Service.

5   'Sunday', Channel 9, 27 August 1995.

## Chapter 10

1   S. de Beauvoir, *The Second Sex*, New York: Bantam, 1952 (original publication 1949).

2   R. Hughes, *The Culture of Complaint: the fraying of America*, Oxford: Oxford University Press, 1993.

3   Max Weber, *The Theory of Economic and Social Organisation*, New York: Oxford University Press, 1947.

4   See, for example, N. Wolf, *Fire with Fire* London: Chatto and Windus, 1993

and R. Hughes, *The Culture of Complaint: the fraying of America*, Oxford: Oxford University Press, 1993.

## Chapter 11

1   D. Ironmonger, *Australian Households: a $90 billion industry*, Discussion Paper no. 10, Centre for Applied Research on the Future, Melbourne University, Parkville, 1989.

2   M. Bittman, *Juggling Time: how Australian families use time*, Canberra: Office of the Status of Women, Department of Prime Minister and Cabinet, 1991.

3   See J. Goodnow and J. Bowes, *Men, Women and Household Work*, Sydney: Oxford University Press, 1994.

4   E. Cox and H. Leonard, *From Ummm . . . to Aha!: recognising women's skills*, Department of Employment, Education and Training, Canberra: Australian Government Publishing Service, 1991.

5   E. Young-Breuhl, *Hannah Arendt, for love of the world*, New York: Vail-Ballon Press, 1982.

6   M. Bittman, *Juggling Time*, 1991.

7   See *Time Use Survey*, ABS Catalogue no. 4153.0, Australian Bureau of Statistics, 1992.

8   E. Diebold, I. Malave and M. Wilson, *Mother-Daughter Revolution: from betrayal to power*, New York: Addison-Wesley Publishing, 1993.

## Chapter 12

1   Warren Farrell, *The Myth of Male Power: Why men are the disposable sex*, Sydney: Random House Australia, 1994.

2   See P. West, *The Australian*, 7 February 1995.

3   T. Lane, 'Terry Lane's Ode to the Common Man', *Good Weekend*, *Sydney Morning Herald*, 15 August 1995.

4   E. Cox, 'A Bedtime Story for Terry Lane', *Good Weekend*, *Sydney Morning Herald*, 23 October 1995.

5   The difference in allocation of resources to men and women has been discussed by Richard Fletcher (University of Newcastle), in numerous media interviews.

6   R.W. Connell, *Masculinities*, Sydney: Allen & Unwin, 1995.

7   A report to the Minister of Education, Training and Youth Affairs, by the NSW Government Advisory Committee on Education, Training and Tourism, *An Enquiry into Boys' Education: challenges and opportunities*, A discussion paper. Chairperson M. O'Doherty MP, 1994.

8   M. Bittman, *Working Life and Family Life: does policy make a difference?*, Canberra: Prepared by the Office of the Status of Women, Department of the Prime Minister and Cabinet, 1994.

9   E. Cox, E. Lintjens and M. Odlin, *Women in New South Wales: a benchmark and exploration of attitudes*, for the NSW Ministry for the Advancement and Status of Women, Roy Morgan Research Centre Pty Ltd, Distaff Associates, December 1994.

10  E. Cox, *A Decade of Women or Decayed Women's Issues*, Sydney: Labour Forum, 1985.

## Chapter 13

1   E. Cox and H. Leonard, *Weaving Community Links: the cost benefits of telephones in maintaining the social fabric through the unpaid work of women*, a project funded by Telecom Fund for Social and Policy Research in Telecommunications, Distaff Associates, Sydney, June 1993.

## Chapter 14

1   C. Lindblom, 'Still Muddling, Not Yet Through', *Public Administration Review*, no. 36, 1979.

2   A. Sinclair, *Working From the Inside: 20 years of the Office of the Status of Women*, Canberra: Australian Government Publishing Service, 1994.

3   D. Osborne and T. Gaebler, *Reinventing Government: how the entrepreneurial spirit is transforming the public sector*, Reading, Mass.: Addison-Wesley Publishing, 1992.

4   M. Sawyer, 'Personal Communication', an unpublished research paper on women and career management carried out at the University of Queensland, 1994.

## Chapter 15

1  H. Garner, *The First Stone*, Sydney: Picador, 1995.

2  E. Diebold, I. Malave and M. Wilson, *Mother-Daughter Revolution: from betrayal to power*, New York: Addison-Wesley Publishing, 1993.

3  A. Sinclair, *Working From the Inside: 20 years of the Office of the Status of Women*, Canberra: Australian Government Publishing Service, 1994.

Chapter 16

1  E. Cox, E. Lintjens and M. Odlin, *Women in New South Wales: a benchmark and exploration of attitudes*, for the NSW Ministry for the Advancement and Status of Women, Roy Morgan Research Centre Pty Ltd, Distaff Associates, December 1994.

2  C. Tavris, *The Mismeasurement of Women*, New York: Simon and Schuster, 1992.

3  J. Baxter, 'The Politics of Housework', in C. Sitka (ed.) *Houseworkshop Papers*, Sydney: Wettank, 1994.

4  Men, however, do between a fifth and a seventh of the unpaid housework that women do, and this does not increase visibly when women are in paid work. So many of the household services are for men whose lives become more comfortable. This is clearly shown in two areas of the time-use study: the first is a near doubling of housework when a husband appears and where there are no children (90 minutes per day to 164 minutes), with children adding a mere 30 minutes for a child under five (E. Cox, WEL media release, 1992 drawing on material from a range of ABS publications).

5  ibid.

6  This information was collected by students participating in the Research Methods II course at the University of Technology, Sydney in 1994.

7  See *Sydney Morning Herald*, November 1994.

8  E. Cox and H. Leonard, *From Ummm . . . to Aha!: recognising women's skills*, Department of Employment, Education and Training, Canberra: Australian Government Publishing Service, 1991.

## Chapter 18

1   B. Friedan, *The Feminine Mystique*, UK: Penguin, 1964.

2   *Time Use Survey*, ABS Cat. No. 4153.0, Australian Bureau of Statistics, 1992.

3   E. Cox and H. Leonard, From *Ummm . . . to Aha!: recognising women's skills*, Department of Employment, Education and Training, Canberra: Australian Government Publishing Service, 1991.

4   P. Leach, *Children First*, Sydney: Penguin, 1994.

5   G. Ochiltree, *40 years of Child Care Research*, Melbourne: Institute of Family Studies, 1994.

6   E. Cox and H. Leonard, *Weaving Community Links: the cost benefits of telephones in maintaining the social fabric through the unpaid work of women*, a project funded by Telecom Fund for Social and Policy Research in Telecommunications, Distaff Associates, Sydney, June 1993.

## Chapter 19

1   E. Cox, *A Truly Civil Society: 1995 Boyer Lectures*, Crows Nest: ABC Enterprises, 1995.

# Index

women's units 133–5, 139–41
women's views, expressing 309–10
Wood, Jan 247, 248–9
work
   evaluating 290–1
   hours of 87–8, 255
   paid, *see* workplace
   part-time 197
   unpaid, *see* household; household
    work

work stereotypes 44, 89, 225–6
working from home 240–1
workplace link with home 239–40,
   296
workplace, women in the 84, 86–7,
   *see also* women in senior
   management
   and household work 83–4, 196–7,
    295, *see also* household
Wyndham, Susan 106–7